SAILING: A Parent's Handbook For Junior Sailing

by

Susan D. Artof

The Center Press
638 Lindero Canyon Rd. Suite 331
Oak Park, CA 91301
(818) 879 0854
FAX (818) 879-0806

copyright © 1994 by Susan D. Artof
All Rights Reserved.
This book may not be reproduced
in whole or in part without written permission
from the publisher.

Published by:
The Center Press
638 Lindero Canyon Rd. Suite 331
Oak Park, CA 91301

Publisher's Cataloging in Publication
Artof, Susan D. 1949 -

Sailing : a parent's handbook for junior sailing / Susan Dale Artof.

p. cm -- (Boating made simple)
Includes bibliographical references and index.
Preassigned LCCN   94-070066
ISBN 0-9626888-3-5

1. Sailing.   I. Title.

QV811.A78 1994   797.1'24

QBI94-86

Cover Picture: By Darien Murry
Jason Artof at 12 years of age after winning
the U.S. Sabot Nationals
Cover design by Roger Gordon
Graphic Design by PRESENTATION TASK FORCE
New Vision Technologies Inc.
Copyright Owners For Presentation Task Force Images
Illustrations by Paul Artof
Printed by Delta Lithograph
Printed and bound in the United States of America

10   9   8   7   6   5   4   3   2   1

TABLE OF CONTENTS

Introduction		Pg. 5
Chapter 1:	What To Expect	Pg. 11
Chapter 2:	How to Evaluate A Program and Its Quality	Pg. 21
Chapter 3:	Vocabulary	Pg. 31
Chapter 4:	Sailing Equipment and Safety	Pg. 47
Chapter 5:	The Race By Paul Artof	Pg. 57
Chapter 6:	Winning/Losing and Sportsmanship	Pg. 67
Chapter 7:	Sports Psychology By Claudia Wainer, M.A.	Pg. 79
Chapter 8:	Sailing Fitness For Kids By Chris Camacho	Pg. 87
Chapter 9:	An Instructor's View	Pg. 95
Chapter 10:	A View From A Junior By Lindsay Artof	Pg. 105
Chapter 11:	Sailing Organizations	Pg. 107
Afterword:		Pg. 121
Index		Pg. 123

To The Del Rey Yacht Club and The Marina Del Rey Yachting Community For All Of Their Support Of Junior Sailing During The Past Twenty Years.

INTRODUCTION

Sailing is the type of recreational activity which is both spiritually and physically healthy for children of all ages. Probably because we were created from the waters, we happily return to the water when given a chance. Sailing for children is perhaps one of the last remaining pure freedoms left in a world. A child finds new adventure each time he or she rigs up a boat and sets sail on even the smallest body of water. Sailing allows the child to harness the wind and take flight on a vessel with no restraining lines in the road or sidewalks to navigate. It is that very freedom to be in touch with the essence of nature which is so incredibly exhilarating for both children and adults. The sport is clean, exciting and it teaches self reliance. Sailing knows only the limitations of the vessel and the skipper. However, water presents ever new challenges to our senses and our sensibilities, and it is always important to remain alert when returning to it.

I've chosen to write this book on *Sailing: A Parent's Handbook For Junior Sailing* because of my own experience as a parent watching my children learn about this special world. My husband and I have listened to countless parents discuss their children's sporting activities such as tee-ball, soccer and baseball. Most parents have experienced these sports themselves as children, and they can easily find a field or backyard on any given day of the week to practice with their kids. If they do not physically throw a ball, parents can comfortably sit in bleachers and cheer their young players forward, knowing that a coach is present to accelerate skills and strategy. Unlike these sports, sailing presents a unique problem for parents since many of them have never learned to sail themselves and often feel alienated from the activity. Instead, they rely on what the sailing instructor might send home with the child at the end of the day. For example, although there is a common vocabulary in sailing which sailors seem to understand (although, don't fool yourself -

many do not), most non sailors have no idea what the terms mean. *Boomvang, centerboard, bailer, batten* or *clew* are all common words used out on the water. But, when a child comes home the first day of sailing class to report that his friend was sailing a *flying junior* whose *foot* tore on the last *leg* of the *luff-in*, an unknowing parent might think a catastrophe occurred and call an ambulance. What really happened was that his friend was sailing a two person type of boat called a flying junior and tore the bottom part of the sail called the foot in the last part of a race called a luff-in. Sounds easy when you know what you are listening to. It sounds like a foreign language when you don't.

    As parents struggle to understand the vocabulary of the young sailor, they run the risk of misunderstanding their children's needs. Children will commonly ask their parents for advice or help, and their parents are unable to effectively give it to them. As equipment breaks and tempers soar on both sides, the words turn to demands and they become heated. I have heard children shouting at their parents to bring them boat or sail parts while the parents stand mutely in the parking lot fuming over the humiliation of an 8 year old barking out commands like a Navy commander. This is definitely not fun and understandably out of line! Conversely, parents are guilty of shouting out expectations which are just not developmentally appropriate. Not all kids are able to sail with the same degree of skill at the same time of their life. While one 10 year old may win a fleet championship, the other is happy as can be sailing around in circles. Parents should not expect more from their kids then is realistic. So it is with this need for greater communication in mind that I considered the importance of writing a book directed to parents about the world of sailing at the junior/youth level.

    As both an educator in psychology and a parent of a national champion youth sailor, I understand the importance of communication with children. A child's self esteem depends upon a clear sense of boundaries and values as well as a certain amount of success at something he or she is good at. The more a parent understands about the child's world, the better the communication of these values and boundaries can be and the more pleasure the child can get from their success. Children who do not have a strong sense of self worth may often thrash around their social world and lash out for attention somewhere. In other words, these children may find themselves getting into more and more trouble with both adults and their own peers. It is imperative that children learn how to handle their stresses in productive and appropriate ways and not turn to violence or performance enhancing substances which can only lead to disaster. For this reason, I have included chapters on sportsmanship, sports psychology along with chapters on equipment needs and vocabulary. It is also important that parents understand what to look for in a quality program and I have included a chapter detailing the elements of such a program.

I have asked several experts in their area to write chapters in this book in order to enhance some of this information. **Claudia Wainer, M.A.** is clinically trained in psychology and has specialized in the area of *Sports Psychology*. She is also a champion sailor on both large and small boats, so she comes with specific understanding of what stresses there are on the water. She has written a chapter in this book on *Sports Psychology*. **Chris Camacho** is a professional physical sports trainer who has specialized in personal fitness training for people of all ages. Chris writes about some of the special physical training necessary to help avoid injury and maximize strength when competing. He communicates his unique understanding of specific sports needs in his chapter titled *Fitness For Kids*. **Paul Artof** has been a Principal Race Committee Chairman of Del Rey Yacht Club for several years and is a SCYA trained Race Officer. He is a Commodore of Westlake Yacht Club and has been in charge of races for junior sailors for over 15 years. All of this makes him extremely knowledgeable of race course procedure and management. Paul has contributed a chapter in this book on *Race Course Procedure* to help understand the often complex horns, time sequences and flags which all racing sailors must eventually become comfortable with. **Jason Artof**, age 20, is a **US SAILING** Association certified Sailing Instructor and has sailed in junior programs since he was 7 1/2 years old. He has traveled throughout the United States and Japan, competing in national and international level boat races, winning the doublehanded Bemis Trophy at the *USYRU-Rolex Junior Championships* (this race is now known as the **US SAILING**/*Rolex Junior Championships*) in 1989 and was picked as a member of the first *Youth Rolex Sailing Team* at that time. He brings first hand information about what it is like to instruct young sailors and specifically, what parents might do to enhance their children's experience. **Lindsay Artof**, age 15, has been a member of junior sailing since she was 5 years old and is currently developing her teaching skills so that she may become certified as an instructor. She has been sailing in local regattas for several years and has developed her race management skills making her a welcome member of the Race Committee wherever she goes. She enjoys both recreational and competitive sailing. Lindsay has written a chapter on what sailing is like from a junior's point of view.

Finally, this book is intended to act as a reference guide for those families desiring to go further into the sailing world beyond just a simple summer class. I have devoted an entire chapter to the sailing organizations including the national organization and governance body called **US SAILING** Association, located in Newport Rhode Island. **US SAILING** is responsible for developing the educational, racing as well as training programs for all American sailors, young and old alike. I have included a discussion of the several national and regional organizations which promote high school as well as college sailing along with information about yacht clubs and boat clubs all of which may be useful to readers who are considering becoming more involved with the sport. There is no question that sailing can become a lifestyle in addition to a recreational sport. This book may help to illustrate some of the features of that lifestyle.

This book is not intended to teach anyone how to sail. There are several wonderful books on the market in addition to a good community based sailing program which can be helpful in achieving that goal. However, it is my hope that you as readers might gain a further appreciation of the sport of sailing through increasing your understanding and awareness of what lies in the background. Further, and even more important to me, is the hope that as parents, you might enjoy gaining an increased closeness to your child. Whether you continue to become involved in this sport is not nearly as critical as becoming more involved in your child's world. After all, they do have something quite magical to teach us.

Susan

A fully rigged U.S. Sabot and skipper Marin Diskant sailing downwind in the Ecology Day regatta on Westlake Lake. She is wearing a life jacket, sunglasses and hat as a part of her sailing safety gear.

CHAPTER 1
What To Expect

Today, children are given an opportunity to explore and experience so many more choices of recreational activities than they were able to even a few years ago. It is not unusual for a child to play a different sport each season and maintain a practice schedule of three days per week while still in early elementary school. Football, baseball, soccer, basketball and even tennis all compete for your child's attention and time. Many parents I met while my children were growing up, spent almost every Saturday and most Sundays carpooling their offspring from one game to another, and if there were two or more children playing sports, then the entire family was separated across town.

The truth is, not every child is good at every sport, and some children do not perform well at team sports in any predictable way. Yet, each child has a right to be good at something, and it is each parent's responsibility to help his or her child navigate through the smorgasbord of choices available. Athletics teach children valuable lessons about life such as winning and losing, sportsmanship and confidence. Children with favorable athletic experiences, and this does not mean just winning, develop greater self acceptance and self esteem. Children having negative experiences in competition, which usually include unreasonable coaching or parental expectation, end up losing more then just games or races. They may lose the willingness to compete in a fair game. These children may cheat, lie or just give up. As parents help their children come up with those special gold nuggets of experiences which stretch their talents, they must also add ingredients to their children's confidence. Knowing what the sport is all about and what it demands of its participants, adds to the more positive experiences children and their parents get from recreational activities. So, let us examine what sailing as a sport, both recreational and competitive, is all about.

Recreational Sailing:

Beginning sailing for kids is considered a personal rather than a group oriented activity, even though classes are sometimes conducted on large boats with many people aboard. Sailing classes are usually structured around a group of 20 to 30 sailors, each assigned to a personal boat rigged with only one sail called the *mainsail*. The most common training boats are approximately 7 1/2 to 8 1/2 feet long and there are several different types (classes) of boats used in programs throughout the country. In Southern California, for example, we use several versions of a boat called a *Sabot*. *El Toros* and a homemade boat called a *Seashell* are often sailed in Northern California. The *Optimist*, the most popular class in the world, is used in many other areas of the country (classes of boats sailed throughout the country will be discussed in **Chapter 4**). What makes all of these boats particularly advantageous for training, is that they are light weight and easy to rig with only one sail to adjust which make it easier for the student sailor to learn the most effective way to harness the wind to power their vessel forward (hopefully). Once the skipper has learned to rig and sail their small single person vessel, they begin to master certain *rules of the road* which dictate who may get the right of way when two or more boats meet. Although there are no lines in the water or stop signs at any intersection, boat handling does require a keen knowledge of these special rules in order to avoid disastrous and often embarrassing collisions. As these rules become mastered and fine tuned, the sailor learns other rules which may give him/her an advantage on a race course.

When the sailor has completed a beginning course, and perhaps even an intermediate course of sailing, he/she may choose to sail a boat with more speed and excitement. They may choose a larger and faster single person boat (singlehanded) such as a *Laser* or *Sunfish* or they may chose to sail some of the exciting two handed (doublehanded) boats which many programs supply such as a *Club/Collegiate Flying Junior (CFJ)*, *Laser II* or Club/Collegiate *420*.

These boats are rigged with two sails, a *main* and a *jib*. Sometimes they also make use of a special sail called a *spinnaker* - the colored balloon type sail seen in photographs of sailboat races. People may choose to sail doublehanded (two people) in recreational areas such as at resorts or marinas, or they may begin to compete heavily in the local or national regatta circuit. The choice is up to the families involved. Even though 10-15% of junior sailors become racing skippers, the other 85% to 90% are happy sailing on a Sunday afternoon without worrying about any start or finish lines, race committee instructions or protests.

Finally, young and old sailors alike usually graduate to even larger boats and learn about real seamanship after they can sail in the harbor on smaller vessels. Such skills may include radio usage, medical emergency at sea requirements, navigation, boat handling in heavy weather, and offshore racing. Once a sailor enters this level of sailing, there is no end to the information which can be learned. Sailing is definitely a lifelong recreational activity which goes far beyond the early first lesson on the water. For example, one of the finest American sailors is Dennis Connor, who originally started his illustrious career sailing as a junior sailor in San Diego Yacht Club's Junior Program. He competed in almost every level of racing, finally culminating in the highest honor of international boat racing by winning the America's Cup. In 1993 he began training for the around the world race called the Whitbred Race to be sailed in 1994. When asked why he wanted to encounter the hardships and difficulty of this particular race when he had already achieved the highest honor in racing, he answered that it remains important to him to continue developing his skills as a sailor. So it appears that sailing skills are never fully mastered but only improved over time.

Competitive Sailing:

During early training, young sailors experience the excitement of personal mastery over equipment and nature without the worry of team mate expectation. In fact, it is quite possible to spend most of one's sailing time in non competitive recreation which makes sailing quite unique when compared to soccer, football, or basketball. However, sailing programs usually begin to aquaint skippers with racing activities soon into the session as a way to reinforce certain boat handling skills. Children seem to enjoy working on efforts to maximize their equipment to go faster, and racing allows them to test success against others in the class. Because sailboat racing allows each individual skipper to test their own skills, sailing provides a specific niche for those who find it difficult or uncomfortable playing team sports. There are no pre-chosen positions to play in sailboat racing, and each child is given an equal chance to play the game and feel that they are in control of the situation.

We will take up the specifics of sailboat racing in another chapter, but for now, it should be mentioned that not all children like the win loss orientation of certain structured sailing programs, and it is important for parents to discuss with their child what winning and losing is all about. Many children come home tired and cranky from a day of sailing because it is hard work even though it is fun. Children may feel upset that they lost every race that day or that their equipment broke. They may ask you to go back to the program and tell the instructors not to place so much emphasis on racing skills. Yet, these kids are still learning valuable lessons beyond just winning a race or sailing the fastest. They are learning something important about themselves in an atmosphere of support from trained instructors. Parents may want to take an opportunity to discuss exactly what is bothering the child and help that child cope with the hard work rather then giving up. It is not as important that they win, but that they attempt to win. Even by losing once in awhile, children learn something about their limitations and strengths.

As sailing skills increase, young sailors may chose to become specialized as either a driver (or skipper) or crew (boat handler or tactician). The two person boat like the *International One Design 14*, *Flying Junior (CFJ)*, *Laser II*, or *420* all require strong and supportive teamwork between skipper and crew. Oftentimes, the crew is chosen because of weight or size requirements, and may be an excellent driver in addition to boat handler. Further, the skipper may be more experienced as a crew, but because of certain physical requirements of the particular boat being sailed, must act as driver for the afternoon. It is necessary that both skipper and crew respect each other, and neither position should treat the other as a lesser participant in the race. I have watched crew and skipper fights which have left both children emotionally injured for no other reason then disrespect for what each bring to the race. Team work eventually becomes essential to the sport, and parents might encourage communication between both parties. In addition, skipper parents should treat the crew parents with as much respect as the actual team mates. Many regattas today will make an effort to recognize both the winning crew and skipper with trophies and publicity. But, this is not always the case, and in certain regattas, only the skipper is recognized. Feelings may be further hurt when a crew and family work hard to achieve a winning attitude only to be forgotten by the skipper and family. It is important to consider crewed boats as a team since the boat cannot be sailed by just one person. Everyone becomes a part of the action!

Peter wells and Jason Artof work as a team to prepare their Laser II.

Scholastic Sailing: College and High School

Collegiate Sailing

The governing organization of collegiate sailing in the United States is called the *Intercollegiate Yacht Racing Association of North America (ICyRA).* It is comprised of 199 college sailing clubs and teams organized into seven Districts: Middle Atlantic Intercollegiate Sailing Association (MAISA); Midwest College Association (MCSA); New England Intercollegiate Sailing Association (NEISA); Northwest Intercollegiate Yacht Racing Association (NWIYRA); Pacific Coast Intercollegiate Yacht Racing Association (PSIYRA); South Atlantic Intercollegiate Sailing Association (SAISA); South Eastern Intercollegiate Sailing Association (SEISA).

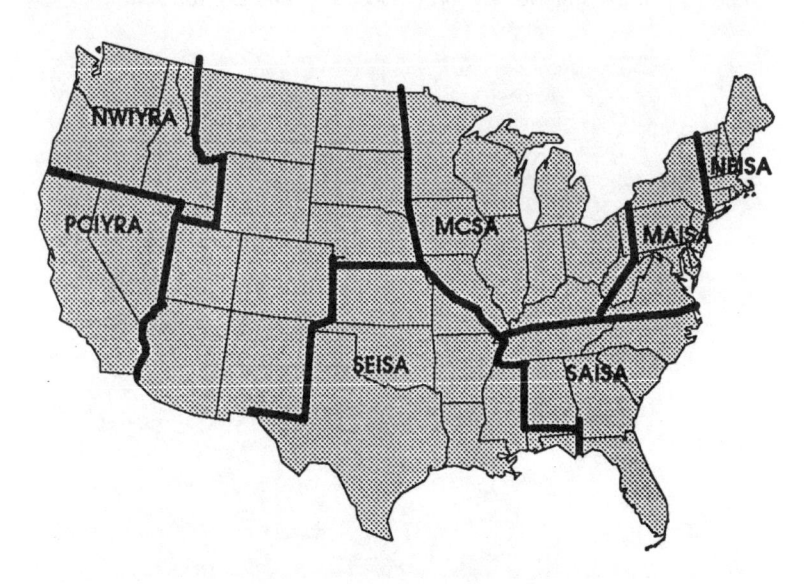

ICYRA Member Districts

At the collegiate level, a full sailing team or program may consist of just a few sailors or as many as twenty or thirty, however, only one representative from each entered fleet, may actually be scored in a regatta. Usually at any college sailing event, there will be an A fleet team and a B fleet team represented for each such fleet. Therefore, even though your child may be on the sailing team, only the top level four or six people may be allowed to sail in a doublehanded event and as few as two people may be asked to sail in a single handed event. However, all teammates are expected to practice between three and five times per week whether they are active regatta sailors or not. As a side note, it is not uncommon for a *rock star* or local champion in high school to enter the college scene with hopeful dreams of becoming an All American, yet be placed on the "inactive" practice squad for the first year while he/she learns the hard lesson of how college sailing differs from club sailing. Sometimes a sailing team's practice schedule may actually interfere with the academic courses the sailor is taking. It is important for the collegiate sailor to keep his/her education a high priority.

The most commonly used boats in college sailing are Lasers for the singlehanded races and Flying Juniors or 420s for the doublehanded events. Boats are rotated through the competition so that any given team cannot win by their equipment alone since every other competitor will get a chance to sail the best and the worst boats. Courses are intentionally short so as to maximize the number of races each day. It is common for 10-15 or even more short races to be sailed during any college regatta.

It is important to note here that as of this writing, there are no scholarships allowed to be offered for college sailing. This is designed to protect the various sailing programs from going on a raiding campaign to recruit the few great college sailors to their program with offers of money. Certain programs are poorly funded while others maintain a war chest of several hundreds of thousands of dollars. Yet, almost every major sailing school can boast of a few nationally ranked sailors on their teams. What happens is that these programs will go off and recruit team members by promising a more relaxed admissions standard. A sailor should choose the campus they want to attend and then look into the sailing program. Good teams will look for good sailors. Small teams will look for sailors. And schools with no team may not care at all. I am including a partial list of colleges which have been listed in the *Sailing World Magazine* as possessing a varsity ranked sailing team during 1993-94. Contact the athletic department at any of the schools listed and you ask for some information about how they recruit.

Boston U	Old Dominion
Brown	Princeton
California State U Long Beach	Radcliff
California State U San Diego	St. Marys
Charleston	Stanford
Coast Guard	Tufts
Conn. College	Tulane
Dartmouth	U of Hawaii
Georgetown	U of Rhode Island
Harvard	UC Berkeley
King's Point	UC Irvine
MIT	UC Santa Barbara
Navy	UC San Diego
New York Maritime	USC
Northwestern	Yale

      Finally, as a word of advice from someone who has paid the tuition and found that college is not a free ride to anyone, coaches may not appreciate the philosophy that school comes before sailing (especially since there is no money in college sailing). A student has only four years of eligibility in any athletic sport including sailing. It is in no one's interest to poke around the campus just to sail the boat - not when a year at the cheapest campus can run $12,000 and an expensive one upwards to $28,000-$30,000. Therefore, sometimes students will be forced to *red shirt* or stop sailing for a semester if their schedules make it impossible for them to participate. Such red shirting is usually allowed from time to time, and a student/sailor might pick and chose what semesters they want to participate the most. The national championships are always sailed in the Spring for example making this the most desired semester to remain on the team.

High School Sailing:

High school sailing is not quite as common as collegiate sailing, but it is gaining recognition quickly and is quite popular as high schools begin to accept the sport as a varsity activity. It is run very much like the college sport with A and B fleets participating at each regatta. However, there is more room for interpretation of regatta structure at each high school event. Parents and juniors should not hesitate to ask their principals or athletic directors if such a program is something which can be developed in the local region. Coaches are often recruited from the colleges and often times clubs will help to donate boats or launching ramps for this activity. For more information regarding high school sailing contact the:

Interscholastic Sailing Organization (ISSA)
Larry White, President
PO Box 397
Niantic, CT 06357
(203) 739-3253

Or Contact **US SAILING** direct at:
(401) 849-5200

The major national High School Championships are as follows:
Cressy Cup   National Singlehanded Championship-
One Person from a high school may qualify through regional championship elimination.

Mallory Cup   National Doublehanded Team Championships
Minimum 4 person team from same High School with an A and a B class participating.

A full rigged Laser sailing in the main channel at Marina Del Rey.

CHAPTER 2
How To Evaluate A Program and Its Quality

Local and national sailing organizations meet each year to discuss program quality issues and develop ways to improve how sailing is taught to both children and adults. From some of these meetings, I have adapted several criteria from which to assess a sailing program's quality. Eight of the most important criteria are: 1) Parent involvement 2) Instructor child ratio 3) Staff training 4) Equipment 5) Effective emergency procedures 6) An organized plan and curriculum 7) Staff ability to be child sensitivity 8) Zero drug and alcohol tolerance.

Parent Involvement:
The best advice I can give parents who are making decisions on where to send their child for recreation, is to become as educated and concerned as possible about the activities of any program whether it is sailing, football, soccer or art class. I am the first to admit that sailing is a sport which keeps outsiders away just by the fact that a sailor goes out on the water and people on the docks cannot view them. Further, as I discuss in **Chapter 3,** sailing uses a special vocabulary reserved for those in the know, again making outsiders unusually vulnerable to feeling alienated and uncomfortable. I have been to many parent child meeting where parents sit outside the main circle of participants and read the Sunday paper rather than projecting any opinions on how to make a program better. I cannot stress enough how important it is for parent's to become an active part of their child's activity, even going as far as getting in a boat themselves and trying it out!

At Del Rey Yacht Club, where I worked with juniors and their parents for more then twelve years, I learned first hand how important it was to get on (and sometimes in) the water with your own child. When my first child began to sail at age 7 1/2, I found that on any given morning, there were parents "hanging" around the docks helping to rig up the rather heavy and cumbersome Sabots (8 foot sailboats) in the program. In those days, the program made it mandatory that a *Parent Of The Day* remain available to help instructors with some of the routine daily problems which occurred. In addition to this *Parent Of The Day*, Wednesday mornings became special as the women of the marina, including members from several local yacht clubs, took to their own boats to sail along with their children. Some of the children actually rigged up their personal boats to loan to their mothers for the morning which made it definitely easier to sail!

I was one of those Wednesday mothers, sailing along in my small boat, often feeling quite out of control. What made this time particularly meaningful to me, was that my child was able to watch me struggle with the very activity he was trying to learn. It gave him added confidence in his own abilities. I may have been older, but he was infinitely more agile and coordinated than me. This became abundantly clear on one particular Saturday when he and I were both racing our Sabots in the SCYA Midwinter Regatta. We had turned towards the finish line, sailing neck and neck, with our boats crashing through the waves (well, maybe there were no waves...only little ripples...but to me they seemed like waves at the time). I was convinced that I was ahead of him until he caught a special gust of wind and sailed on ahead, leaving me eating his spray in the background. What did he do then? He just looked back at me with the widest grin I had ever seen and said, "Good race Mom." All I could feel was pride in his accomplishment. He had beaten a bigger and faster and more skilled parent. I obviously had nothing left to teach him in racing. There are few recreational activities where a youngster can out perform their parent by age 10 years of age!. To help parents understand what it is like to sail a small boat, today, at Del Rey Yacht Club, we conduct a special Junior-Senior race for parents to compete with their kids just so that they can experience some of this pleasure - or pain for themselves.

Parents who drop their children off at the sailing program, only to reappear several hours later, are often bewildered about their child's fears and concerns or even discipline problems. Further, these parents are rarely able to anticipate equipment needs and often the missing or broken equipment causes a child to have a "bad" day in the program. The more successful young sailors usually have a parent or two nearby and somewhat available during the day. Even with the working schedules for many families, a parent can either help with their child's boat in the morning or at the end of the day. Furthermore, they might choose to work with their child on the water after program hours. At Del Rey Yacht Club, we host evening activities several times per week and encourage parents to come by and watch their children sail. The main purpose is to encourage parental involvement and communication.

Things To Look For In A Program:
Ratio of Staff To Student
Programs with the best reputations make it a point to staff themselves with enough personnel to maintain safety and security at all times. Although some programs feel that beginners and advanced sailors can sail together and help with some of the staffing problems, it is recommended that there is more staff for beginning sailors then for advanced ones. Del Rey Yacht Club makes an attempt to use a ratio of *one* staff member for every *five* sailor, *one* staff member for every *eight* intermediate sailors, and *one* staff for every *ten* advanced sailors. Various programs maintain different ratios. It is important to ask how many students are enrolled and how many staff are expected to be available each day, and then ask what the general mix of sailing skills will be within the overall program. Remember, beginners take more time and require more personal staff attention then the advanced sailors do. Consider your child's special needs when picking a program.

The staff is usually made up of a *Head Instructor* along with several *Regular Instructors* and some *Assistant Instructors*. The total number of staff depends upon the size of the program. For 10 sailors, there may be only two instructors. For a program of 15-20, there may be three or four instructors. If the program is 25-30 at least five instructors and perhaps some trainees called CITs may be expected. Use your judgment and ask questions regarding the staffing of the program you are most interested in.

Staff Training
Currently there is a special Instructor Training Certification program which sailing instructors are encouraged to take before they are hired by most quality programs. This training program is administered by **US SAILING Association (See Chapter 11: Sailing Organizations** for more information regarding this National Governing Organization). The first level *(Level 1)* of instructor training begins with a comprehensive four day program designed to teach experienced dinghy, windsurfer, and/or keelboat sailors the basics of how to teach beginner sailors. The next level *(Level 2)* course emphasizes instruction on how to coach racing strategies to more experienced young sailors. Both levels require a rigorous in class and on the water performance standard which is tested before certification is given. The Head Instructor, of any quality program, should have a minimum of *Level 1* training plus several years of teaching all levels of sailing. All other Instructors and Assistant Instructors should also have the minimum *Level 1* course completed or be in the process of such training. Today, insurance companies are using the amount and quality of instructor training as part of the risk assessment when rating the policies of sailing programs and clubs. Although, no amount of training can absolutely assure against all accidents, **US SAILING** Instructor Training can help minimize the potential for such problems and assure some standard of quality in instruction..

Along with a minimum of *Level 1* training, make sure that all of the staff is Red Cross Certified for CPR and First Aid. This is mandatory for **US SAILING** Certification, but you may find some staff who are not certified *Level 1*. Be sure to ask if they are at least *CPR* and *First Aid certified*.

Some programs make use of CITs or Counselor In Training personnel to fill their staff needs. These young junior sailing instructors, usually 13 and over, have been successful in their own racing program, and are ready to further their skills by teaching others. As long as these young teachers are also taking further classes and are well supervised, they make great assistants to any program. In fact, one of the finest junior programs in the country, *San Diego Yacht Club*, hires one junior instructor for every regular instructor and they are of tremendous help to the older instructor staff. These CITs are not eligible to be *Level 1* certified since **US SAILING** requests that their trainees be at least 18 years of age. Ask your program's director about such staffing. I would not recommend that the majority of staff be CIT.

Finally, some large programs have the luxury of hiring a full-time *Program Director* to supervise the entire program. This person is usually older than the rest of the staff and may be a credential teacher or certified coach who is working the program during the summer. Then again, this person may be a full or part time employee of the yacht club or community based program whose sole responsibility is to administer all of the paperwork and scheduling needs of the program. A Program Director is a luxury which many programs just cannot afford. This does not mean that the program is not a quality one, but it may mean that you have to look to the club membership for the person who is really in charge. Most yacht clubs will choose a member to become the *Junior Activities Chairman or Coordinator*. This person volunteers their time and is devoted to the development of such junior sailing in his or her harbor. Because of their personal interest in the sport and the program, this person may be even better equipped to handle all of the program needs then even a paid staff member. I can speak from some experience on this subject since I was such a volunteer for twelve years, and I met so many other people just like myself, all around the country. Most of us had children in the program at one time or another, and we had a vested interest in making the program work.

Equipment

For your child's safety it is important that a program maintain the following equipment at all times:

1. <u>A well stocked and usable first aid kit (**See Chapter 8: Fitness For Kids for a list of the bare minimum for such a kit**), located in several places throughout the area where your child may be including:</u>
    A. in the classroom or instruction area
    B. at the pool with the lifeguard
    C. out on the water in at least one chase boat with each group

2. <u>An adequate number of working *chase boats* or patrol boats working with each group of sailors.</u> These can be small 12-15 foot power boats (the Boston Whaler™ is a common boat of choice for this purpose) with strong motors. It is preferable that there is chase boat for each sailing group which goes out on the water so that if there is a beginning group and an advanced group sailing in the afternoon, the program should provide *two* chase boats. If there are three levels sailing, then there should be *three* boats patrolling. Sometimes, different skill levels may share a chase boat if they remain in the same general area, but it is hard to maintain order when too few chase boats are available, especially if the different skill levels begin to spread out on the water.

There should always be *two* instructors in each boat so that one can drive while one can assist in rescues. These boats should have motors which are well maintained and always working. In addition, adequate floatation devices should be aboard for all passengers. Finally, instructors should not take students aboard these boats for fun, and should only use them when conducting actual classes. Failure to follow this rule could jeopardize the entire program with the Coast Guard since drivers of boats with passengers may be required to have a Coast Guard License to carry passengers.

3. <u>An adequate number of radios or communication devices such as telephones available both on and off the water</u>. It is sometimes necessary to quickly contact an adult on the dock, especially if the program is conducted far away from the shore. A marine type radio or other two way radio, is very important. In some harbors, sailors may be three or more miles away from their home base, and immediate communication ability is essential for safety.

4. <u>Enough blackboards for the instructors to use when gathering their students for the morning and afternoon chalk talks</u>.
These talks are an instructor's only way of communicating valuable information to each student before they actually go out on the water to practice.

5. <u>Enough loud hailers for each instructor to call out instructions on the water.</u>
There should be enough batteries available to keep these hailers working at all times.

6. <u>Is there shade available if the sun is too strong? Is there some extra emergency sunscreen available if the child forgets to bring their own?</u>

7. Are there <u>lockers or spaces available for safe keeping of personal objects such as lunches or spending money?</u>

A Well Designed Emergency Plan
1. An emergency plan should include a signed medical release which is available to the program supervisors and instructors at all times while your child is in the program on or off the premises. This means that even when your child is traveling to regattas and you are not there, an adult should have a copy of your medical release available in case of an emergency. Besides giving *authorization for emergency medical treatment,* these forms should include *the name of your doctor, the preferred hospital* if available, *your insurance policy number* and of course *any allergic medical problems or unusual medical needs. The form must be signed and dated for it to be valid.*

Because of the great liability problem plaguing our country today, most clubs or community programs go to great extent to include a copy of liability release to go along with the medical release. Although there have been very few claims concerning Junior sailing, it is appropriate to discuss this with your attorney if it concerns you.

2. There should be an adult available on the premises of the program with the emergency numbers of the local hospital and paramedic units. It is also important that numbers for medical helicopter service and the Coast Guard are also quickly within reach, especially if sailors are sailing far away from the actual clubhouse facility.

3. When at all possible, a program manager should be on the premises and available to quickly administer these emergency procedures when needed.

4. In earthquake regions, such as in California, an earthquake preparedness program including emergency supplies, should be available and personnel should be trained to implement the procedures. This may mean that adults near the program should be available to act in assistance when necessary.

An Organized Plan Of Curriculum
1. Are there bulletins coming home telling you the parent what plans are expected during the upcoming week? Is there a calendar of events planned far enough ahead so that there will be no surprises for either you or the staff?

2. Do the instructors know what they are supposed to be doing each day?

3. Are there staff meetings planned throughout the week where staff discuss plans for the future? Do any of these include parents? They do not have to, but sometimes it is nice for parents to discuss children's needs with the staff in such meetings.

4. Is there a variety of activities to keep even the most hard to please youngster interested? Is there a mixture of racing, fun, and social events planned throughout the program? Are there rainy day activities?

5. Is there too much *down time* for your child so that they get bored or is there too much active time so that they may get too tired?

6. Does the program have a specific and enforceable discipline standard? It is recommended in most programs that a code of standards be signed by both child and parent before engaging in the program activities. If a child does not adhere to this code of standards, then it is appropriate to call the parent and send the child home. Parents must understand that a program such as sailing, cannot accommodate children who become difficult to manage in a group. Because of safety concerns, it is important to maintain a level of cooperation

A Staff Which Is Child Sensitive and Parent Sensitive
1. It is assumed that the instruction staff is well trained, but do they understand about child development such as how children learn and play?

2. Is the staff capable of talking directly to each child?

3. Can the staff discuss the child with the parent?.

4. Are there problems in **staff conduct** which the child might discuss frequently? Take some of this seriously and talk with the Program Director or Head Instructor. Do not let things "just go away" because they really never do! Sometimes children may exaggerate situations when they are having difficulty adjusting to the program standards and requirements, but sometimes these concerns turn out to be quite real and they should be worked on. Take a moment each day to ask your child how their day went. Listen to both what they say and how they say it! Sometimes their words are not as important as their overall facial and body expressions.

5. It must be understood, that most sailing instructors are relatively young and are not professional teachers, but, they should always act professionally. Be prepared that they may make some mistakes and be reprimanded for them, but, all staff should be respectful of parents as well as the children they are teaching. If problems are suspected, contact the *Head Instructor* or the *Program Director* to discuss them.

<u>Zero Tolerance For Drugs And Alcohol</u>
Alcohol and drug use should never be tolerated anywhere or at anytime children are present. In addition, the instructors should never tolerate your child's use of such substances. Be aware that there are some (although not many) programs where such drug use is common, and parents should be quite concerned! I recommend that parents thoroughly check out all programs regardless of the alleged reputation.

CHAPTER 3
Vocabulary

A-C FLEET - Sailors are traditionally grouped into skill level fleets with C fleet for beginners, B Fleet for intermediate and A Fleet for the most experienced sailors. Usually the competitors themselves know what fleet they are best suited to sail, but written and even unwritten rules governing certain classes of boats may put some limitations on how long a person might be able to sail in a lower skill fleet. For example, in Sabots (Naples version), sailors move into the most advanced Sabot A fleet when they win both a one day regatta and a two day regatta where there are more than eight or more other competitors from at least two different clubs. In the Laser class, a competitor moves into the A Fleet after winning two regattas with at least five competitors sailing at the event.

ABEAM - At right angles to the centerline of the boat.

BAILER - A container used to remove water from a boat. This is required equipment aboard most small dinghy boats such as Sabots This can be made from an old bleach bottle (keeping the cap tightly sealed) with its bottom cut out. On Lasers, the bailer is inserted and attached to the bottom of the boat and automatically bails the boat out when it fills with water.

BALLAST - Weight which has been placed in the lower part of a boat to give it stability.

BATTEN - The thin wooden or fiberglass slats used for sail support when inserted into sewn pockets **(Batten Pockets)** on the edge of the sail (usually the main). See **Sail Parts**.

BEAM - The width of a boat at its widest part.

BEAM REACH - The point of sail with the apparent wind coming at right angles to the boat.

BEATING - Sailing as close to the wind as possible. Same as **Close Hauled or By The Wind**.

BECALMED - No wind at all. This is one of the most uncomfortable conditions to sail in and takes extreme concentration.

BEFORE THE WIND - Sailing in the same direction as the wind. The wind fills the sails from behind. Same as **Running**.

BLOCK - The official nautical term for a pulley. The metal or wooden shell (**cheek**) acts as a housing for one or more grooved wheels (**sheave**) which acts as a pulley. Two blocks with a line through them forms what is known as a **tackle**.

BOOM - The horizontal spar which supports the sail by holding the sail foot.

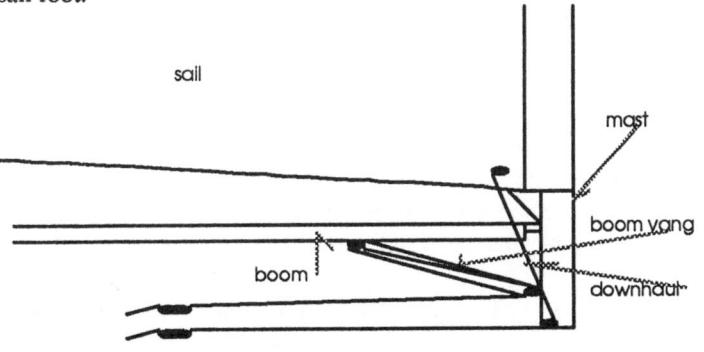

Boom Vang and related parts

BOOM VANG - A wire or line running from the boom to or near the bottom of the mast which holds the boom. This serves to lower the risk of an accidental jibe and helps provide better sail shape when sailing off the wind.

BOW - The forward part of a boat.

BOW LINE - The docking line on the front of a boat. Called a painter on most dinghies.

BREAKWATER - A manmade structure used to break the force of waves at the mouth of a harbor. Races sailed outside the breakwater are considered open ocean races and will be more challenging with waves and current than those races inside the breakwater.

BROAD REACH - Sailing with the apparent wind coming over either quarter of the boat.

BULLETS - A racing slang term used for first place in a race.

BUOY - A floating aid used for navigation and is also used for sailboat rounding during races.

BURGEE - Each yacht club has a unique emblem displayed on a flag known as a burgee. When sailing for a yacht club you sail *under their Burgee*. People like to collect these from clubs where they sail.

BY THE LEE - sailing with the wind behind the boat but blowing from the **leeward** side (the same side where the boom is) of the sail. This can cause the boom to fly over uncontrollably to the other side of the boat an action called an **accidental jibe**.

BY THE WIND - Sailing close hauled or beating. See **Close Hauled** or **Beating**.

CAPSIZE (Turn Turtle) - To turn over in your boat (it happens to all dinghy sailors). Turning turtle is when the boat is completely upside down in the water. Sailors of small boats quickly learn how to right their boat and continue to sail.

CAT BOAT - Boats with only one sail with the mast set well forward (Sabot, Laser or Sunfish).

CENTERBOARD - A blade projecting through the bottom of the hull in the center of the boat which pivots up and down into the centerboard trunk of the boat. It is used to keep the boat from sliding sideways in the water in the same way a daggerboard or leeboard does.

CHUTE - A slang term for the spinnaker sail.

CLASS - similar boats which are grouped together such as the Optimist, Sabot, Laser, or Sunfish boats. Class boats are maintained with specific building requirements known as one-design class rules so that all boats of a class are as identical as possible. To avoid unnecessary surprises, make sure you know about all the rules of your particular class before competing.

CLEAT - The fitting on which a line can be secured.

CLEW -The outermost, lower corner of the sail. See **Sail parts**.

CLEW TIE DOWN - Lasers and certain other classes have a line which goes through the grommet (reinforced hole in a sail) on the clew and around the boom.

CLEVIS PIN - A pin used to close the U in a **shackle** (U Shaped connector to permanently or temporarily connect things) or to connect to a **turnbuckle** (a fitting used to adjust tension on standing rigging).

COMMITTEE BOAT - The boat from which a race is conducted.

COME ABOUT - Steering the boat so that the bow comes through the eye of the wind and the boat moves from one tack to the other. Steering the other way creates a **jibe**. See **jibe**.

COURSE CHART - A piece of paper handed out at a race which tells which buoys or marks boats should go around. Each course chart contains several courses from which the race committee will chose to send the racers. Skippers should become familiar with these courses prior to actually racing. The chart should be pasted to the inside of the boat using duct tape and a water proof bag so that it can be referred to throughout the race.

COTTER PIN - A small pin slipped through the end of a clevis pin to secure it and keep it from sliding. See **Clevis Pin**.

DAGGERBOARD (DAGGER BOARD) - Similar to a centerboard serving the same purpose. Unlike a centerboard, it is removable slides up and down instead of pivoting up and down. It is used in Optimist, U.S. Sabot, and Laser boats among many.

DNF - In sailboat racing this means that a boat did not officially finish the race and is therefore not counted as a finishing boat even if the skipper has sailed the entire course. This may happen as a result of equipment breakdown, lack of wind or sailing the wrong course.

DNS - A term in sailboat racing for a boat which does not start a race. A regatta is made up of several separate races, and if for some reason, one of which is not sailed, the skipper will then receive a DNS as the official score for the separate race in that regatta. Also see **PMS**.

DOLLY - a special light weight trailer used to transport boats in and around the parking lot or storage yard by pushing or pulling. These are not used for towing, but can be brought in addition to the towing trailer. Dollies are recommended to take when competing in large regattas where there will probably not be enough club dollies for everyone.

DOWNHAUL - A line attached to the tack of the sail which pulls the sail down the mast. See **Sail Parts** and **Boom Vang**.

DRY SUIT - A loose fitting one piece outer wear vinyl suit with tight fitting thick vinyl seals around the neck, wrists and ankles used to protect against cold. It does not let any water in at all, and is mandatory wear in places where the water is unusually cold. May be worn all year around in certain regions. See **Chapter 4: Sailing Equipment and Safety**.

DUCT TAPE - A gray durable water resistant tape which is easy to tear and is indispensable for quick repairs while on and off the water. A must for every gear bag and tool box! See **Chapter 4: Sailing Equipment and Safety.**

FAIR - Used to describe the smoothness of a boat's hull. The more fair the boat, the faster it is. Skippers will often sand their boards and the boat bottom using wet-dry sand paper to remove any bumps.

FOOT - The lower edge of the sail. See **Sail Parts.**

FOUL WEATHER GEAR - Protective outer wear used to prevent the sailor from getting too cold. One piece suits are good for junior sailing when the sailor is not expecting to capsize. Dry Suits are used to keep all water out even when the sailor is in very cold conditions. Wet Suits are tight fitting rubber suits (either short or full length) which let in a thin layer of water which warms when close to the skin surface and is used when sailors are frequently in the water. Ask the program director what conditions are like in the region you are sailing. Experienced sailors will quickly steer you in the right direction. See **Chapter 4: Sailing Equipment and Safety.**

GHOSTING - Silently sailing in almost no wind. This is especially beautiful at dusk when the waters are still.

GOOSENECK - Hinged fitting on the mast which connects the boom to the mast. Should keep an extra one in the toolbox when dinghy sailing.

GROMMET - A metal ring in a sail which allows lines to be connected to the sail.

GUDGEON - See Rudder.

HAIL - To call another boat over. The race committee may hail boats to come nearby in order to pass on instructions.

HALYARD - See **Running Rigging**.

HEAD UP - Turning the boat into the wind. The opposite of **HEADING OFF**.

HEADER - To head off or away from an original intended course because of a wind shift while the boat is sailing close hauled (beating).

HEADSAIL - The sail set forward of the main mast. It may be a jib or spinnaker in small boat sailing.

HEAD OF THE SAIL - The top corner of the sail. See **Sail Parts**.

HEAD TO WIND - The boat's bow is directly into the wind.

HEEL - When the boat lies over at an angle while sailing.

HIKING OUT - The action of stretching the body over the edge of the hull to help keep the boat flat and counteract the heeling while sailing close hauled.

HIKING BOOTS - Thick vinyl boots which are reinforced along the top designed to assist sailors by strengthening the ankles. Foul weather gear is usually tucked into the boots to create a water tight seal. See **Chapter 4: Sailing Equipment and Safety**.

HIKING PANTS - Specially designed pants with padded leather patches on the back which are used to support a sailors thighs while hiking out. Most commonly used by Laser sailors to give them more strength and endurance and to save money on worn wet suits and shorts. See **Chapter 4: Sailing Equipment and Safety**.

HIKING STRAP - A strap placed in the soul or bottom of a dinghy for a sailor's feet to slip under while hiking out.

HULL - The actual body or shell of a boat without the rigging.

INSPECTION PORT - A hole in the hull of a boat, commonly found in Lasers or on the **thwart (center seat)** of Sabots. It is used to allow skippers to reach inside to check fittings (bolts) and to even store gear such as food or light weight jackets. These are handy to include in your boat when possible.

JIB - The forward smaller triangular sail.

JIBE (GYBE) - To turn the boat away from the wind where the **stern (back end)** of the boat passes towards the eye of the wind while running.

LEE - To be on the downwind side. To be in the lee of an object is to be sheltered by it.

LEEBOARD - Hangs off the side of a boat and pivots up and down (Naples sabots use these) and acts like a daggerboard to prevent side motion.

LEECH - The outside edge of the sail. See **Sail Parts**.

LEEWARD - The side away or opposite from the wind.

LEEWAY - Sidewise slipping motion of the boat away from the wind caused by the wind.

LIFEJACKET - **(Personal Flotation Device or PFD)** Required to be worn properly by all juniors in most programs. The vest type of jacket is acceptable if Coast Guard Approved. See **Chapter 4: Sailing Equipment and Safety.**

LINE - A rope on a boat chosen for different functions.

LUFF - The forward edge of the sail. See **Sail Parts**.

LUFFING - To describe the sail when it is shaking back and forth because the boat it pointed into the wind.

LUFF-IN - A name given to certain informal regattas in many regions.

MAIN - The mainsail or largest sail attached to the mast. See **Sail Parts**.

MAINSHEET - A line used to control the boom and the mainsail. Each type of boat requires a different length of such line depending upon the length of the boom and size of the mainsail. A little more than 3 times the length of the boat should provide ample length for the mainsheet. Line should be thin enough to fit through all of the blacks easily, yet thick enough to cleat properly.

MARINE TEX™ - A particular brand of putty used to permanently fill small cracks and holes in boat hulls and boards.

MAST - Vertical spar which supports rigging and sails.

MAST TUBE - The sewn sleeve in a sail where the mast slides.

MAST STEP - A shaped brace (usually placed into a molded area of the hull) where the bottom of the mast fits. This should be checked periodically since the stresses of sailing may actually weaken the surrounding hull and cause cracking.

OAR - A paddle used to row or steer a boat. A ping pong paddle or a purchased small oar may serve this purpose. This is mandatory equipment on certain small boats to help skippers move away from danger when their sails are not powering the vessel.

OFF THE WIND - Sailing to leeward. Opposite of **ON THE WIND**.

ONE DESIGN - Classes of boats which are built to strict rules assuring that all boats of a class are as similar as possible. Sabots, Optimists, Lasers, and Sunfish, are all one design classes.

OUTHAUL - An adjustable line or wire used to secure the mainsail to the back of the boom.

PAINT PEN - A permanent marker which marks on any surface is useful to label gear.

PINTLEs - See Rudder.

PMS - In sailboat racing this is a slang term for a Premature Start which means that boats have crossed the startline before the sounding horn or gun. Such a start means that the boat will be given a disqualification (**DSQ**) unless the skipper restarts the race according to the official Racing Rules.

POINT OF SAIL -The direction a boat is moving in relationship to the wind.

PORT - Refers to the left side of the boat. This also refers to the direction a boat is sailing. Port tack means that the wind is coming over the port (left) side of the boat.

PROTEST - An appeal of a sailing rule infraction. When one sailor thinks that another sailor(s) has violated such a rules, the sailor may appeal by submitting a written protest to a part of the race committee called the **Protest Committee** which will conduct a formal hearing of both parties before issuing a decision. **See Chapter 5: The Race.**

PURCHASE - A system of leverage used to move an object. To get is to create purchase.

RATCHET BLOCK - A large block in the center of the boat used to better control the mainsheet.. These blocks have a clicker on them.

REGATTA - A series of races (usually five or more) over one or several days.

ROACH - The amount of curve designed into the back of a sail. See **Sail Parts**.

RUDDER - A flat blade hung from the transom used for steering. **Pintles (pins)** are inserted into **Gudgeons (eyes)**. Pintles and gudgeons occasionally stick or bend and tools should be made available in the toolbox to help separate these if needed.

RULES OF THE ROAD - Safety regulations which govern the lakes and oceans so that boats can move safely through these waters. Racing rules make use of these rules to establish a safe and competitive sport for all to enjoy. See **Chapter 5: The Race**.

RUN - To sail with the wind behind the boat.

RUNNING RIGGING - All wires and lines which are hauled on to handle the sails. This includes the **Halyard** (used to hoist a sail up the mast); a **Sheet** (used to control and tighten or loosen sails depending upon the wind direction; a **Topping lift** (used to support the weight of the boom when the sail is lowered) a **Clew Outhaul** (controls the tension of the foot of the sail; a **Downhaul** (used to tension the luff of the sail).

S HOOK - A heavy duty hook used to permanently connect one end of something and easily connect the other end with the top part of the S.

SAILING INSTRUCTIONS - Instructions prepared by the race committee and handed out at each regatta telling the sailor the schedule for the day, the starting order for the race, and any special rules which will be followed for that particular regatta. Most regattas are sailed under the US SAILING rules, but amendments will be noted in the sailing instructions. See **Chapter 5: The Race**.

SAIL PARTS - Sails are used to power the boat and each part of the sail has its own special name. Sail makers work with sail cloth and the design of each section of the sail in an effort to create the fastest sails.

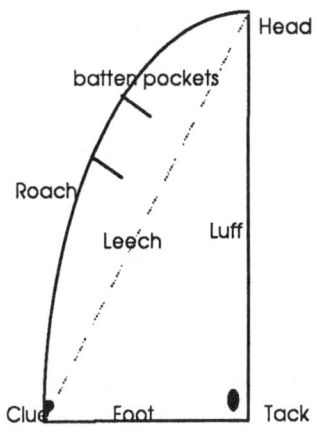

Sail parts are the same from a mainsail or jib

SHACKLE - U-shaped hook used to permanently or temporarily connect things.

SHEETS - Ropes (lines) used to specifically control the sails.

SINGLEHANDED - Sailing alone in the boat. **DOUBLEHANDED** refers to sailing with one other person acting as crew. Larger boats may be sailed with more than two crew.

SKIPPERS MEETING - A short meeting scheduled before each regatta where instructions for the day's event will be handed out and discussed. These meetings are sometimes mandatory and some representative (it may be the parent) should be present to receive any information which might be vital to the day's performance. See **Chapter 5: The Race**.

SNAPSHACKLE - A hook with a spring loaded safety catch across the end.

SPINNAKER - A lightweight, three cornered sail which is used for running (down wind sailing). Often multiple colored and flying like a parachute in front of the boat, the spinnaker is controlled by using a pole and sheets from each clew.

SPONGE - Recommended equipment on some boats to mop up water which can make the boat very slippery and uncomfortable while sailing.

SPREADERS - Horizontal struts attached to the upper part of the mast to help increase the strength of the shrouds which hold up the mast.

SPRING CLIP - Used to secure the rudder in place and keep it from floating upward. The spring clip is pressed in to remove the rudder.

STANDING RIGGING - All rigging and hardware which is used to support the mast and keep it upright and straight. Standing rigging ncludes **Shrouds** (supports the mast from side to side) and **Backstay** (supporting the mast in the back to prevent forward movement)) and **Forestay** (supporting the mast in the front to prevent backward movement).

STARBOARD - Refers to the right side of the boat. It also refers to the direction (**tack**) the boat is sailing when the wind is coming over the right side (**starboard**) of the boat.

STERN - The back of the boat.

TACK - Refers to the changing direction of the boat when the bow passes through the eye of the wind. See **Port and Starboard**.

TACK - The lower front corner of the sail.

TANGS - Metal strips used to connect the boom to the gooseneck.

TILLER - The handle by which the rudder is controlled.

TILLER EXTENSION - A hinged extension of the tiller which allows the skipper to control the rudder from a distance while hiking out or sitting forward in the boat. These are premade and can be purchased for each type of boat sailed.

TOW LINE - A line which is thrown to a competitor from a chase boat or committee boat and is used to tow the sailor to or from the venue.

TRANSOM - The flat part of the back of the boat.

TRAPEZE - A support used by the crew to enable them to hike far out and away from the actual hull and to gain extra weight to counterbalance the heeling motion of the boat.

TRAVELER - A rope, rod or track running across the boat on which the block carrying the sheet slides back and forth.

WINDWARD - Moving towards the wind. **Opposite of LEEWARD.**

WAKE - The visible trail of water off the stern of the boat. Wakes from other boats might cause turbulence and may be a cause of capsizing.

WHISKER POLE - A spar used to extend the jib while running.

For an excellent reference book on sailing vocabulary, look for the book:
   Sailing as a Second Language: An Illustrated Dictionary by Fred Edwards, International Marine Publishing Company, 1988.

Sailing upwind on a bright summer's day.

CHAPTER 4
Sailing Equipment and Safety

In sailing, equipment becomes important both for its durability and its safety. This chapter will discuss the types of boats most frequently sailed as well as some of the equipment needs for the junior sailor. In addition, I have included a discussion of important traveling tips for the competitive regatta sailor. Performance and safety are dependent upon the condition of the equipment which is used. Parents should frequently check with their child about any broken parts or pieces which need to be replaced. The child's entire sailing experience will be so much better if everything works as it is supposed to.

The Boat:
To begin with, active junior and community sailing programs will have already chosen a particular boat to sail based on a certain set of criteria and then ask students to either bring their own such boat to the program, or else charter or borrow a boat directly from the program. If purchasing your own boat, expect the prices to vary from $200 to $3500 depending upon the class and newness of the boat. I recommend asking the Program Director if any boats are available on the used market or if boats are provided in the program for the beginning sailor. For example, Westlake Yacht Club offers both options to the sailor with a discount given to those who bring their own boats. At Del Rey Yacht Club and California Yacht Club, kids are asked to bring their own *U.S. Sabots* and *Lasers* while the doublehanded *CFJs* and *Laser IIs* are provided free as part of the program. At King Harbor Yacht Club, the junior program uses equipment which has been purchased by a special Youth Foundation, but there are restrictions on when that equipment can be used. It is best to check with various yacht clubs in the harbor regarding boat

acquisition. Club bulletin boards and harbor local newspapers are both great sources to check for boats. However, be prepared to call immediately if you see something interesting.

As discussed in Chapter 1, beginning sailing classes use a simpler boat which is less physically demanding, while more advanced training is conducted on sophisitcated vessels which require working with two or more sails. Training boats are usually chosen for their lightweight and simple rigging. These boats usually have extra safety features such as foam-core rudders and hulls which remain floating when capsized. They are also easy to repair and capable of taking a fair amount of abuse from the beginning sailor as he/she develops the necessary skills to advance to the more advanced boats.

Training boats:
The most popular training boat is *The International Optimist Dinghy*. There are over 300,000 of these easy to rig-easy to sail small boats on the water in more than 50 countries. The class is strong and the one-design sailing rules which govern what you can or cannot do to the boat, are strictly enforced. For more about this class and its development in the United States, write to:
Joni Palmer
Optimist Class Administrator
1187 Green Holly Dr.
Annapolis, MD 21401

As popular as the *Optimist* is in Europe and other countries of the world, it has not succeeded in winning over every region of the United States and there are several other well established classes of boats which have been developed over the years. This makes it hard to choose a single official entry level boat for the entire country. For example, in Southern California there are two well established and rule run classes of a boat called a *Sabot*: *The Naples Sabot (leeboard)* and the *U.S. Sabot (Daggerboard)*. In addition, there is a third class of *Sabot* called the *Winward Sabot* which is considered to be a developmental class of boat built independently in garages and without the strict class rules governing the other fleets. Another small training boat is the *El Toros* which is sailed in Northern California and looks like a *Sabot*. In the southern coastal waters of the United States, many beginning sailors learn to sail on a boat called the *Sunfish*. The *Sunfish* is bigger than an *Optimist* or *Sabot*, but its sail is easier to bring down while on the water making it especially good to sail in areas where storm conditions quickly develop unannounced. Finally, efforts are being made for the larger and more advanced *Lasers* (discussed in the next paragraph) to be equipped with a smaller rig, called a **radial rig**, which enables the boat to be used as both a beginning and an advanced training boat. The radial rig include a smaller Laser mainsail and mast section which is designed to make the boat easier to sail for smaller and lighter people. The problem with using boats for dual purposes is that they are often too heavy for younger children to move on and off the docks. The smaller and lighter boats discussed above are probably the ones you will see while looking into singlehanded programs.

Advanced boats:
        As children grow older, they usually outgrow the smaller singlehanded training boats. In the *U.S. Sabot* class, kids begin to talk about being too big when they reach 120 lb. Yet, they may be too small for the next size singlehanded boat such as the *Laser* which a weight of 160 lb. or more is recommended for optimum performance in competitive fleets. The radial rig *Laser* can be sailed well by sailors 105 lb.-150 lb. *Lasers* are very popular in most of the country and in college sailing. Another boat, *The Europe Dinghy* was developed in Europe to accommodate the medium sized sailor as well as women. The boat is best sailed by people under 155 lb. (135 lb. is a good weight for this boat) and is presently used as the Singlehanded Women's Olympic boat. The *Sunfish* is also a favorite program boat because of its rigging and simplicity of boat handling, although it is not as exciting to sail as the Laser.

        The Laser II is a two person high performance sailboat rigged with two sails (main and jib) and which requires a high degree of skipper crew coordination because of its trapeze and spinnaker requirements. It is a boat which needs constant upkeep and care to remain competitive and has developed a reputation for being temperamental, however, it is a very exciting boat for kids to sail and has been chosen by **US SAILING** to be the Youth Championship boat for the last several years because of the high degree of boat handling skill necessary to sail it. The thrilling *International One-Design 14* is the Formula race car of sailboats. Its speed and unusual rigging make this a demanding racing boat used by the "Top Gun" of programs. The *420 (Club/Collegiate or regular)* is another two person boat which has been chosen by several national regatta selection committees and collegiate programs on the East Coast. Typically, the collegiate versions are more reinforced in the hull and come with untapered masts *420s* are a popular two person boat on the East Coast, Canada and Europe and can be sailed with or without trapeze and spinnaker. The *Flying Junior (FJ or CFJ)* is similar to the *420* and is sailed extensively on the West Coast and by many of the major Collegiate sailing programs throughout the country. The collegiate version *FJ* is similar to the *420* in that it is more reinforced and the mast is untapered. The *470* is another doublehanded boat sailed in some programs as well as chosen as one of the boats ailed in the Olympics. This is a more exciting larger cousin of the *420*, but is more sensitive to breakdown and hull damage. Other boats which may be found in programs include *Larks*, *C-Scows*, *Y Flyers*, *Holders*, *Tasers*, *Luders*, *Fireballs*, *Techs*, *Shields*, *and Solings*. If a particular boat has not been mentioned here, I apologize. As you might see, there are almost as many different classes as there are programs.

Program boats are not always the most exciting boats to sail once the junior sailor has developed advanced skills. Sometimes harbors will encourage "family owned" boats to participate in a racing program in order to encourage both adults and juniors to interact. *The Snipe* is one such two person boat which has remained popular throughout the country as a boat the entire family can sail. Families will trade off crew and skipper positions for years in this class making it one of the great family boats ever. Then there are the three person boats which clubs use to encourage big boat skills. *The Lightening, Thistle, Shields and Flying Scott* are just four of the many varieties of these open cockpit boats. *The Santana 20*, *The J-22* and *J-24* are but three multiple crew closed cabin racing boats which are sailed throughout the country in very large fleets. These boats are trailerable but heavy and require dry (out of the water) storage.

Fortunately, the major championship regattas will select their competing boats and try to announce these decisions in time for programs to develop an early training plan. Boats vary considerably in rigging and sailing characteristics, and kids need time to practice on a particular type of boat. Many of the major regattas will provide the boats and even time to practice for a day or two prior to the actual regatta.. It is important to read all announcements carefully and keep in touch with the championships by reading *American Sailor Magazine,* the official **US SAILING** magazine.

Depending upon where the boat is stored, the removable equipment from the boat should be secured each night. This means that the tiller, centerboard, lines, sail, clips, blocks, or anything else removable, should be put into some protective bag and either brought home or locked away to protect against theft. Even the mast and sails should be secured.

Personal Equipment:
Besides the boat and its equipment, every junior sailor should maintain a bag of extra personal *stuff* which should be brought to the program each day. This includes:

> *A change of clothes including a bathing suit*
> *Bucket and sponge for cleaning and bailing*
> *Extra line to use as tie down or replacement*
> *Extra parts for the boat which frequently might break (ask the instructors of your program for a list)*
> *Foot wear (waterproof Aquasocks™ or similar type)*
> *Hat (baseball type is just fine)*
> Knee pads (get at a hardware or paint store to protect knees)
> *Latest version of the US SAILING Racing Rules*
> *Paddle (for smaller dinghy boats this is usually mandatory)*
> *Paper and pencil for notes*

Spending money
Sunglasses (to protect the eyes against sun damage)
Sunscreen (PF 15)
Towel
Water bottle
Whistle
Duct Tape

    A Coast Guard approved *life jacket* is mandatory equipment for most programs. The most common and comfortable such jacket is the vest type jacket made by Omega™ or other similar manufacturer. These jackets zip in the front and should be worn at all times while on the water even if a wet suit is also worn. Besides saving one's life in case of an accidental injury, the added buoyancy is quite helpful when trying to get back into a capsized boat. Your sailor might not wear the jacket if it is not comfortable, so make sure that the jacket is easy to get on and off and is not overly confining.

    For Laser sailors, *hiking pants* are seriously recommended for both comfort and clothing protection. These are specially designed pants with padded leather patches on the back. The pants are used to support a sailor's thighs while they are hiking out while going upwind. These pants are used to give added strength and endurance to the sailor as they sail in heavy air. In addition, the pants save money on worn wet suits and shorts which are always ripped apart in just a few wearings by the rough deck.

    In addition to the above equipment, there are some specialized clothing requirements for sailing in cold weather or water. Since *Hypothermia* (a critical lowering of body temperature) is a serious health hazard when exposure to unusual cold occurs, all sailors should remember to protect against such conditions. Dressing in layers is recommended for increased warmth and flexibility. Although only bathing suits are worn under wet suits, warmer clothing can be worn under spray suits, windbreakers and dry suits. Socks should be worn under sailing boots to help protect the feet from cold and blistering as well as to aid in removal of the boots. See the glossary of terms in **Chapter 3: Vocabulary** for further explanation of these personal safety suggestions.

A wet suit - This rubber suit should be worn if capsizing for long periods of time are expected. Laser sailors often wear this protective clothing.

Spray suit - Lighter than a wet suit, this clothing may come in one or two pieces and be worn over existing clotting for warmth and protection against spray. It should not be worn if the sailor is going to get very wet since the suit is not water tight.

A dry suit - Does not allow any water in and can be used in especially cold water areas such as on the East Coast during winter or the Great Lakes most of the summer. This suit is quite expensive, but is necessary for full outer protection in adverse conditions.

Sailing gloves - made by several manufacturers, these leather gloves protect hands against blistering and wear when grabbing lines. Recommended for anyone sailing Sunfish, Lasers, or any smaller boat for long periods of time or in heavy wind.

Sailing boots - All young sailors should wear protective waterproof footwear such as Aquaboots to protect against stubs, bruises and cuts. For advanced Laser sailing, high top rubber boots made by Douglas Gill™ or Aigle™ (or any similar manufacturer) is recommended to add strength to the ankles and help with hiking.

Hat over ears - In very cold climates, it is recommended that a lined hat with ear protectors be worn even in summer if the conditions warrant such clothing.

Travel Toolbox:
For the traveling regatta sailor, a complete toolbox should be developed and transported for every race. The following suggestions are adapted from an article by Brian Weeks which was reprinted in *American Sailor Magazine (Dec. 1992)*. Although it appears from

this list that you may be expected to bring your entire house and garage, most of these items are small enough to fit comfortably into a plastic toolbox (tackle box). Our family has been caught without some of these items in the past, and the results can be disastrous. Think ahead and your racer will benefit.

1. A small tack hammer for quick release of rudder pintles which get stuck or hammering pins back into place when they come undone
2. Phillips screw driver (medium sized)
3. Pliers
4. Medium regular screw driver
5. Adjustable wrench (medium)
6. A putty knife
7. 1" chisel
8. Two Box wrenches. Check your boat for the standard size you need
9. A battery operated drill and all its bits
10. Tube of silicon to fix bailer leaks or other fitting leaks
11. Sandpaper for repairs and fairing the bottom hull and boards. Use wet-dry 600 paper for this work
12. Marine Tex™ or Bondo™ works for repairs
13. Small plastic boxes for storage
14. West System™ repair pack and small amount of fiberglass cloth.
15. Black electric tape
16. Duct Tape
17. Extra assorted lines for quick repair
18. Spare bolts and screws and washers for rudder and gooseneck
19. Extra cleats and blocks and stern plug (if needed)
20. Pop Rivet™ gun for quick repair of mast parts
21. Swiss Army Knife or general rigging knife
22. Matches or cigarette lighter for burning the ends of line

Finally, when traveling to a regatta, boats may be transported by using a trailer or the roof of a car (called car topping). If you decide to car top the boat, carefully secure all tie downs. Do not use stretchable line, and stop often to recheck for loose ties. Many of us who have traveled have watched with horror as a boat flies from the car onto the highway. It only takes one instant for this disaster to happen, and it is preventable. Trailers make it easier to transport some of the larger boats. These trailers may be home made with wooden storage boxes built into the structure to accommodate boards, line and sails. There are some very creative trailers at every regatta. But again, make sure the tie downs are securer and the electrical connections are working in the hitch assembly. Also, make sure that your car and hitch are strong enough to tow both the boat and the trailer. As a last word of caution, read your motor vehicle code and drive in the slowest two lanes to avoid any unwanted tickets!

A Laser tied down to a customized trailer.

Laser IIs are rigging up on the beach at Gulfport Yacht Club during the Nautica/US SAILING Youth Championships.

CHAPTER 5
The Race
By
Paul Artof

So, now that Johnny knows something about how to find the wind and keep his boat moving in a forward direction, he might decide it is time to enter his first race. He tells you that he is to be at the water's edge on Saturday morning at 9:30 AM. You ask him what he needs and he shrugs. You ask him how long it will take, and he doesn't know. You ask him whether you should stay at the race site, and he turns on the television. So, what are you supposed to do? You don't even know if you should pack a lunch for him or give him spending money. And, what about medical help if he hurts himself? Does anyone know anything? Well, let's see if we can eliminate some of this confusion.

The Race Day

Preparation
A parent is the first level in the organization of the young sailor. When my son began to compete, it became important to plan ahead and make sure that appropriate clothing and parts were brought. Although we tried to encourage our young sailor to be personally responsible, it was important to be a major part of the planning. Parent's may help in the preparation phase of race day by making sure to bring most of the following items. If your region requires more specific things to bring, include those as well. (**See Chapter 4** for a more complete list):
1. Change of clothing
2. Life jacket

3. Sailing gloves
4. Stern Plug -somehow they are frequently missing when we get to the boat
5. Extra line
6. Lunch, snacks and lots of water - if they will be offshore for a long period of time
7. Some extra spending money so they might buy a drink or candy bar or make a phone call

<u>Rules</u>

Although it may not look like it from the water, there are specific rules which govern a sailboat race. It often amazes me that my children were able to learn them and grasp their meaning. The first and most basic level of rules and guidelines are published by **US SAILING**. These rules are compiled by the **International Yacht Racing Union (IYRU)** and are adopted by the *United States Sailing Association*. These rules cover almost everything and certainly are well worth being familiar with. A copy of these rules can be obtained from **US SAILING** whose address is located in **Chapter 11** of this book. While you are at it, if you join this association, a complimentary copy of these rules comes along with your membership. **Also see Racing Rules below.**

Assuming that your young sailor has had prior sailing experience, it is worthwhile to review these sailing instructions and rules as part of the race day preparation. Such advanced review has two advantages. The most obvious is that even if you are not fully familiar with these rules, and your child cannot explain one or more of the notations on the sailing instructions, you can encourage him/her to ask for help. This accomplishes the second benefit. You are now in a position to learn more yourself as your proud junior sailor comes back and explains the rules to you.

Events for young sailors are typically held in One Design boats. This means that all the boats racing in a certain fleet are all the same. Behind each type of One Design boat, is an association which makes rules which govern the way the boat is built, rigged and sailed.

It is essential for optimum success to obtain a copy of these unique rules before entering any one design race. I have seen many good natured and willing parents help their children repair or rig a boat such as a Laser or FJ only to be disappointed by a competitor who protests (see **Protest** below) the race results due to specific one design rule noncompliance. This protest may be as simple as using a wrong manufacturer of a block or putting the sail numbers in the wrong place on a sail. Some class boats are more rigid in their interpretation of the rules than others and everyone should be encouraged to know about these rules.

For many races, the Race Committee will write out additional rules which augment the official **US SAILING** rules. These are called **Sailing Instructions**. The committee may wish to add to, modify or eliminate some of the rules that are provided by **US SAILING** or the One design class. If there is a conflict, these sailing instructions override all of the previous rules. These instructions are likely to be unique to a particular Yacht Club or racing event and it is important to be sure to review these with your young sailor before each race.

Just prior to the race day, the race committee will gather all of the competitors into one area to give last minute instructions or to make last minute changes in the Sailing Instructions. This is typically called the **Skippers Meeting**. You are encouraged to attend. This is the last time that the sailors can discuss the race with the race committee. Consequently, a good time to ask questions. Any changes at this time supersede any earlier rules or instructions.

Race Course
At the time of the Skippers Meeting, all competitors will receive instructions **(Race Chart)** as to what the race course will look like and where it is located **(the venue)**. Often, transportation to this site is provided by the race committee with the use of a long rope **(tow line)** pulled behind a small power boat. The tow line should be tied to the foot of the mast. The mast can better handle the stresses of being towed than the other fittings on the boat. Competitors will sail their

boats up to this tow line, grab on to it, and then get a free ride out to the start line. Except for the first time, when some kids are confused by the procedure and may actually fall out of their boats (the tow boats always stop and help when this happens), most sailors enjoy this part of the race day. Of course, if the race is sailed nearby the clubhouse or dock, the sailors will sail directly to the venue. The race course is defined by three or more strategically placed marks or buoys. Based on the location of the starting line, one mark will represents a course for sailing up wind **(The Beating Leg)**, one course sailing down-wind **(The Running Leg)**, and a course sailed perpendicular to the wind **(The Reaching Leg)**. Some possible race course patterns are shown below:

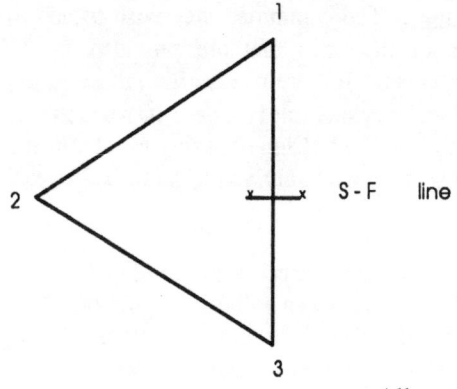

All courses begin at the Start - Finish line (S - F)
Possible courses could be:
A. Start, 1, 3, Finish
B. Start, 1, 2, 3, Finish
C. Start, 1, 3, 1, 3, Finish
D. Start, 1, 2, 3, 1, 3, Finish

There are a couple of augmentations that could be added to the above course selections.

1. Twice Around: Sail the prescribed A, B, C, or D course twice usually beginning the second rounding by sailing through the

Start - Finish line. The race committee would select this option in the event that the wind velocity was adequate strong. This option would lengthen the race.

2. *Reverse:* Conducted by sailing the above selection of courses by reverse sequence. That is, by beginning the race by sailing mark 3 first. This course would be conducted if the wind were to reverse direction.

The Beginning of the Race

After all of the boats have arrived at the start line, the Race Committee checks to see that all boats are accounted for. **It is very important to inform the race committee if your child will not be at the start line regardless of the reason.** This could be because of an injury to the skipper or malfunction of the boat If the committee is unaware of the situation, it could delay the start of the race or cause a search to begin. In this case safety boats may be deployed to look for missing sailors instead of looking out after those on the water.

The sounding of a **horn blast (or whistle)** and the raising of a white shape begins the starting sequence of the race. This shape could be a wind sock or a flag and is sometimes called a **cone**. The shape and design may have been covered in the skippers meeting earlier. There is usually 4 minutes before this flag is lowered, and one more minute before the next on is raised (total of five minutes). The raising of the first flag is a way that the Race Committee announces *"on your mark."* Five minutes after the white shape is raised, comes a blue shape *(get set)* and after five more minutes the red shape is raised *(Go!).* This entire sequence between the raising of the white shape and the raising of the final red shape takes ten minutes. As part of this ten minute sequence, there is a traditional one minute period between the lowering of each shape and the raising of the next. Every time a shape goes up, there is a sound which is typically an air horn or whistle, but sometimes a gun or cannon blast is used.

In many dinghy races which have several fleets racing, to speed up the sequence of starts, a race committee may favor using a three minute time interval between shapes. In this case, the white shape comes down two minutes after it goes up. One minute later, the blue shape is hoisted. This sequence continues on as the red shape is raised and the first fleet starts. When there are additional fleets, then two minutes later the red shape comes down. One minute later the red shape comes back up and the next fleet starts. Each additional fleet starts in the same manner every three minutes. Usually the fastest fleets begin racing first keep from sailing through the slower fleets.

The Race Has Begun

It is so hard to be a parent and watch your child in one of their first races. All of that commotion out there with boats going everywhere and there is your child sailing his/her boat with sails flapping helplessly, behind a bunch of other boats which are sailing sharply upwind. What happened? What happened is not nearly as important as what you do about it. Many parents inadvertently fully humiliate their child by shouting out advise or criticism. It is probably best to remain silent until your young sailor returns to the dock. At that time, be cool and ask how it went. It is amusing but painful watching non-sailing parents confronting their sailing children and trying to offer advise. If you fit this classification, it is best for you to ask the sailing instructor to interact on your behalf. This accomplishes two things. 1) The child will take the advise more seriously without straining the relationship with you and 2) You may be incorrect in your observation and remedy which may only confuse your young sailor. Worse, you may precipitate an argument between you and your child or you and other parents on the dock! Now that's humiliation.

Race Rules (Rules Of The Road):

At this point, I will cover just a few rules which might help you to understand the sometimes complicated nature of a sailboat race. There are a lot of racing rules set forth by the *International Yacht Racing Union (IYRU)*, and made available by **US SAILING**. Some of the rules change every four years and very sailboat racer should have the most recent rule book.

Right of Way
1.   A port-tack yacht shall keep clear of a starboard tack boat.
2.   When on the same tack or jibe, a boat upwind will keep out

of the way of a boat downwind.
3. When on the same tack, A boat behind will keep out of the way of a boat ahead.
4. When coming from behind and passing on the downwind side of a boat that is ahead, the boat passing will initially allow the other boat an opportunity to stay out of its way.

Protest

The above mentioned rules are just a fraction of the plethora of rules your young sailor has learned or will eventually learn while sailing in an organized program. There is no shortage of ways to break the rules. As you will notice in sailing, there is no umpire. There is no one individual who makes sure that the game is played fairly. In place of an authority figure, sailing makes use of peer surveillance, a system which usually works quite well.

We stress to our children the concept of right and wrong. We are proud of them when they do the right thing on their own. It brings both of you honor. Consider being in the heat of competition and accidentally breaking one of those many rules. You are in first or second place; will you still be honorable and disqualify yourself? Hopefully the answer is yes and sailing competition is based upon the honor of this concept. But, to prevent against the possibility that such infractions are not reported, the official sailing races have a built in law enforcement system. When Johnny breaks a rule and does not disqualify himself or accept an alternative penalty, Ernie can immediately indicate to Johnny (using official procedure as described in the rules) that he saw the incident and will report him. Ernie initiates this action by telling the Johnny that he is **"Protesting"** him. If he doesn't know Johnny personally, or if in the heat of competition, he cannot make out who the skipper is, Ernie can possibly identifying him by the number on Johnny's sail. Once this happens, Johnny must accept or deny his responsibility. This is a measure of Johnny's sportsmanship. All of this takes place moments after the infringement. Let us suppose that Johnny accepts the guilt. If an **alternative penalty** is provided for in the sailing instructions, then you will probably see Johnny sailing two continuous 360 degree turns **(called a *720*)**. This is usually the penalty for breaking a sailing rule although in some races, the penalty may only be one such turn *(360)* or no alternative penalty is allowed at all. The race committee will have decided upon the nature of their penalty system prior to the race and will discuss this at the skipper's meeting. Your son or daughter must check the sailing instructions and listen carefully in the skippers meeting to determine what the operating penalty system is. It's too late once the race has started.

If Johnny does not think that he broke any of the sailing rules, then he will continue on as if nothing happened. Ernie has now displayed *a red flag* **(protest flag)** on his boat which will remain there for the rest of this particular race. This indicated to Johnny and the Race Committee that Ernie intends to *Protest*. Once Ernie has completed the race, he will sail up to the Race Committee boat and tell them of the protest and who it is against. The Race Committee will convene a Protest Hearing at the conclusion of the regatta. Each skipper is given an opportunity to tell their side of the story and have witnesses appear with their viewpoint. The Protest Committee will allow or disallow the Protest once all of the evidence is heard. Johnny will be allowed to count his score in the race in question if found not to have broken the rules. On the other hand, if found guilty of the infringement, he will then be disqualified and given last place or worse.

Racing is a sport of honor. It prepares your child to be a citizen in the adult world. A word of caution to parents regarding protests. It is alright for parents to listen and support their children in this process for most races, but, there are other levels of championship regattas where parents must not be anywhere near their child immediately after the race. Most race committee protest hearings will discourage active involvement by the parent during the hearing, and it is important to help your child learn the protest procedure so that they are comfortable in the hearing room as either a witness or defendant. Although not always welcomed, protests happen to just about everyone at some time.

Scoring

A regatta is usually made up of more than one race. It is most common for the score in each race to be same as the finishing position. This is called the **low point scoring system.** Second place gets two points, third place gets three points and so on. First place deviates a little. The first place boat receives 3/4 points. This gives a little advantage to the first place finisher and a hardship to the race committee now has to add in fractions. Adding the points in all of the races gives the final score. The boat with the lowest overall score will win.

For more information regarding racing, look for the following books:

Advanced Racing Tactics, Stuart H. Walker, W.W. Norton and Company Inc, 1976.

Championship Tactics, Gary Jobson, Tom Whidden and Adam Loory, St. Martin's Press, 1990.

Sail Power: The Complete Guide to Sails and Sail Handling, Wallace Ross, Alfred A. Knopf, 1975.

Sail To Win Series published by International Marine. (several books written by different authors on the subject of racing and tactics.

US SAILING International Racing Rules, Adopted by United States Sailing Association, 1993-96 rules.

Winning in One-Designs, Dave Perry, Dodd Meade and Company, 1984.

Cooperation between sailing friends while rigging a Sabot during the summer sailing program.

CHAPTER 6
Winning, Losing and Sportsmanship

Show me a good loser in professional sports and I'll show you an idiot.
 Leo Durocher
 Baseball Manager

Defeat is worse than death, because you have to live with defeat.
 Bill Musselman
 Basketball Coach

Out of the 1994 national sports headlines comes a chilling story of misaligned competitive values. Olympic figure skating hopeful Nancy Kerrigan is assaulted after her practice and is unable to defend her National Figure Skating Championship title, a supposedly necessary step to be named for the 1994 U.S. Olympic Team. Her chief rival, Tonya Harding, skates to victory and secures a berth on the Team. Later, it is revealed that Tonya's bodyguard and husband may have been involved with hiring a hitman to break Kerrigan's knee cap in order to keep her from competing. Arrests are made and a dark shadow is cast over the sport of figure skating.

In interviews with other skaters it is revealed that it is not unusual for skates to be sabotaged, music tapes to be lost or destroyed, or threats to be made just before a competition. Most of this is done to young children on their way up the competition ladder. It seems that kids can have crazy parents willing to do almost anything to assure their champion darlings some success. What might a 23 year old desperate competitor do when they have lost almost everything else in their lives but their sport?

In a recent sports broadcast, the sportscaster begins by reporting a story about uncontrolled fighting on the basketball courts. This is followed by a discussion of the usual technical fouls in the hockey rink and a story about the increased disturbances on the baseball diamond. At the end of the sports hour, the newscaster shakes his head and asks an unseen audience, "What ever happened to just plain old sportsmanship?" A good question to ask Nancy Kerrigan who continued on her path to the 1994 Olympics despite her injury, but who will never forget her ordeal, however many championships she skates. Her life has been altered forever. If we could, we might ask this question of Leo Durocher, Bill Musselman (see the quotations at the beginning of this chapter) or any of the modern day professional coaches who believe in winning at all cost.

It is obvious that professional sports has become excessively expensive to maintain. It can cost over $40,000 per year to become an Olympic skater, which is perhaps the motivation to play hard and play for keeps. But, should winning override decency? I am afraid that we are passing this *win at all cost* message down to our young athletes even before they have chosen professional sports. If winning is for winners, and losing is for jerks, then what about the 99% of the athletes today who are willing to work hard to excel at their sport with all that they have to give regardless of the results? Should they just pack up and go home? And what about the winner today when he or she loses tomorrow? How will they cope with that? Can a tennis player win every game or a swimmer every race? Do players resort to cheating because they cannot stand going home and living with the pain of their defeat?

Tonya Harding had a great year in 1990 but an inconsistent 1991 and 1992 when she placed fourth (after reporting almost a week late to the Olympic training camp) behind the third place Kerrigan in the Winter Olympics. Then in 1993 her personal life disintegrated and she slid to a disappointing fourth place in the national championship. Going into the 1994 Olympics, she was not considered to be the front runner. Nancy Kerrigan was. Did Tonya Harding have anything else in her life to help give her identity besides her skating? Or, did those who supported her believe that she needed the added protection for her ego or worse, for theirs? The true motive for Kerrigan's assault may never be known, but the results we do know. Physical and mental assaults on competitors hurt everyone in athletics -- skaters, skiers and sailors along with hockey players, football players and baseball players -- all of us are assaulted when players cheat to win.

Parents are a strong influence in their children's perception of themselves in relationship to others on the playing field. For example, a little league parent who sends the message to their child (even nonverbal) that he/she will only be loved if they win, is really setting the child up for a lifetime of failure. Why? Because that child soon learns that winning at all cost is what matters most. These children perceive that winning is equated with love, and they also learn that a good attitude, self respect, and honor are of little value. Eventually, someone who is younger, faster, or stronger challenges the ability of this performance compulsive competitor, and the result may be to turn that person towards performance enhancing substances or cheating behavior to ensure the win. I've seen kids blatantly and unapologetically cheat in a race and ignore the rules or bully their way past other competitors. When confronted by someone in authority, the child too often replies that "Everyone does it; so why shouldn't I?" Or "I don't see what's wrong with it as long as you don't get caught." Then there are the kids who feel that they just cannot relax without one more hit on their hand rolled joint or snort of white powder. Great stuff, we're teaching our kids. Let's for a moment, examine how this win at all cost attitude can develop in even the youngest or most talented youth.

Winning, Losing and Self Handicapping:
Is it possible for a winner to set himself up to lose? This is the question Steven Berglas and Roy Baumeister raise in their book *Your Own Worst Enemy* (Published by Basic Books, $21). Berglas and Baumeister suggest that it is common for people who are highly successful and perhaps even obsessed with success and winning, to engage in self destructive behavior that assures them an increased chance to lose. They call this phenomenon **self handicapping** and it occurs even more when these success oriented people are confronted with increasingly tough competition. In other words, as people

become more and more used to winning, they develop an increased fear of losing. As a result, they establish unconscious credible excuses for their loses in order to save face. In Joannie M. Schrof's review of *Your Own Worst Enemy*, in the May 17, 1993 issue of *The U.S. News & World Report,* she suggests that, "It is often success that leads people to flirt with failure." I've seen this type of self handicapping in sailing many times. A champion sailor is late for a regatta because his car runs out of gas. The equipment on a chartered boat breaks down due to a simple malfunction which could have been avoided if it had been checked carefully in the morning. A young sailor about to sail his first advanced fleet race wakes up with a bad stomach ache and cannot compete or just sleeps in too late and cannot get to the start line on time. Each of these excuses effectively keeps the winner from having to really face the competition. How convenient. "I lost because of _____." You can fill in the blanks with anything. The disappointment of the lose is lessened because there is a credible excuse. But, what would have really happened if they had actually raced.

Now, if the competitor is really terrified of matching themselves against the newest threat, then how do they continue to compete? A successful young sailor, who has been raised to believe that they are only as good as their publicity, may take on ever more dangerous handicaps such as drinking or other major drug use in order to *relax* and *loosen up*. The danger of this is usually obvious to everyone but the user. If one loses a race while high, and is sloppy at the start or hits a mark during an upwind maneuver, they can pass off the loss to being tired or just not *on* that day. Their equipment failed them (they were too high to check it); their competitors were stupid; the Race Committee was untrained; the race wasn't important; the party went on too long; who cares about this dumb race anyway. This is the classical pattern of self denial.

Although occasional rationalization (excuse making) is an important part of coping with stressful situations for all of us, the chronic user of self handicapping never learns how to get back into the winner's circle fear free. We have all read about major league baseball stars who fall from grace because of drug use, and we have asked ourselves how a player making $12 million can throw it all away? These players have never really learned how to get back up from defeat, and they choose to run away rather then risk to win. Well, it appears that non-professional players can also throw away their futures because they fear losing more than anything else. To quote one of the parents I used to spend time with on the docks.

> *"You can't win unless you risk losing."*
> *Lois Good*
> *California Yacht Club*

I couldn't agree more with this. Even the most talented national champion will one day find someone behind them trying to take away the title. Kids must learn how to take the risk of losing in order to become winners in life.

Sportsmanship:

Sportsmanship: "One who exhibits qualities especially esteemed in those who engage in sports such as fairness and self control." (American College Dictionary)
"A person who is fair, generous a good loser and a gracious winner." (Webster's 9th New Collegiate Dictionary)

In analyzing the above definition, sportsmanship, is really about developing **self esteem** and **moral behavior**. A child who feels good about him/herself can sail through life as a winner no matter what the win/loss column in the sports page reads. There is no question that winning in a competitive sport feels great - perhaps one of the greatest feelings a young person can experience. But, learning how to conduct themselves as socially graceful people, both on and off the competitive stage, is the key to a lifetime of success. Fairness, graciousness, self control are all part of this conduct.

Can one learn to be a sportsman without losing the competitive spirit? Leo Durocher may not think so, but **US SAILING** sure does and recognizes sportsmanship when it is present. Today, it is quite common for programs and organizations to hand out special sportsmanship awards and incentives during the end of the year trophy presentations. However, I might question whether or not we actually value these awards as much as the first, second or third place winner's trophies. I have heard kids who have won some of these high honors laugh self consciously about them and say that they are not real awards anyway. They feel that they are consolation prizes. How far from the truth can this be. If anything, we should value sportsmanship above any other awards. These sportsmen should be considered our role models. So how do we as parents elevate sportsmanship? We must value it as well.

Self Esteem and Sportsmanship:

Parents may help to develop the value of sportsmanship in their children by increasing both a child's self esteem and moral behavior. Here are some reminders in a list I adapted from the *National PTA* and *March of Dimes Joint Parenting: The Undeveloped Skill Project* several years ago. In lecturing and talking to parents about these reminders, I am always surprised by how many parents just forget that their children are indeed just children.

Eleven Steps To Better Self Esteem:

1. Show respect to your child and allow for individual action within a given limitation.

2. Define and enforce limits and rules and communicate the family value system clearly. Let the child know what is expected of them.

3. Reward each child when possible-verbally as well as with action. Praise, recognition or special privileges are often good rewards for a good job.

4. Take your child's ideas seriously. Listen to them. They make sense more often then you might think. Don't put the child down just because their ideas seem different from yours. Discuss where they developed their beliefs and why

you cannot agree with them. Often, what you may hear gives you clues to their fears and concerns.

5. Have reasonable expectations about what they can or cannot do. Understand that there are age differences in development and punishment should be age appropriate.

6. Help your child to develop tolerance for their own actions and those of others. Help them to understand and accept differences in people and help them appreciate strengths in others as well as themselves.

7. Remind them just how special they are-even if they do not win!

8. Be available for them even if they chose not to take advantage of it all of the time. Being there is still important to them.

9. Tell them you love them irrespective of their performance.

10. Give them increasingly more responsibility appropriate to their age.

11. Let them fail in order to let them win.

Moral Behavior and Sportsmanship:
Developing morality in children is also a parent's responsibility. This requires *parental communication (talking), modeling, and reinforcement of appropriate behavior* in what I call the TMR model of morality development: Talking, modeling, and reinforcement all combine to help children learn acceptable behavior which translates to sportsmanship.

Talking: Talk to your child about moral and ethical issues which matter in society. Include in that discussion issues related to winning and losing.

Children cannot be expected to pick up morality and ethics without having a forum in which they can express their concerns regarding the inconsistencies of life. Moral development progresses from a very concrete and simplistic view of doing the right thing in order to protect oneself from pain and punishment (avoid getting in trouble because I will get punished), to a more abstract and complex understanding of what is right which encompasses the ethical needs of society (I will rescue this person at any cost because life is more important than the event). Children (and sometimes adults) need help in moving through this concrete to abstract thinking and behavior. When adults are available to communicate a higher standard of moral thinking to a child who is thinking at a less developed level, research has clearly shown that profound changes take place in the child and they take on more of the adult actions and thoughts. The more dialog, the more change.

Modeling: Be a role model for your child and demonstrate appropriate moral behavior at home for the child to imitate.

Learning theory has long demonstrated that children model what they see and hear at home. "Monkey see and monkey do" is quite true when looking at parent-child interaction. It is a demonstrated fact that modeling of poor social behavior, even on the television, encourages poor social behavior. Children have come home after only a few days at a new school with new friends, acting entirely different then the week before. A father or mother who is a bad sport in their games, will no doubt convey this way of behavior to their own children. If we worry about TV cartoons or video games doing damage to our children, what do we think our own behavior as parents might do to a child?

Reinforcement: Reinforcement of appropriate morally based behavior will lead to better self control and more advanced emotional development.

Reinforcement is actually defined in psychology as anything which increases the chances of a behavior being repeated. Reinforcement may be either positive or negative. A **positive reinforcement** (such as praise, food, money or privileges) encourages a child to conduct their behavior in order to seek more of that reinforcement. "I like it", "I want it", and "I'll do more to get it"! A **negative reinforcement** is an unpleasant stimulus which is actually quite unattractive to the child and which is avoided if at all possible. It is not punishment, which is painfully inflicted when we do something wrong in order to get us to stop a certain behavior; but rather, a negative reinforcement encourages us to do a desired behavior in order to avoid the unpleasantness surrounding us. For example, ignoring a child who is having a temper tantrum is considered to be a negative reinforcement rather than a punishment. This is because the usual result of ignoring the child, causes him/her to cease the tantrum. Evidently, the lack of social response by the parent is so unpleasant, that the child is actually encouraged to do something to stop the lack of attention...in this case, to stop the tantrum. Negative reinforcement appears to work far better and for a longer period of time than punishment since giving the child any attention at all, including punishment, only rewards the child for their action. A child's poor sportsmanship may be treated with either direct punishment or withholding of team attention by the coach and other team mates.

Most children enjoy pleasing their parents and seek these reinforcements. The overriding principle in reinforcement is **CONSISTENCY** in when and how such reinforcement is to be used. Once a parent creates a priority of expected social and emotional behavior for their child, the parent must maintain some sort of consistent schedule so that the child can really learn what is expected of them. Further, each parent must agree on the type and amount of such reinforcement. This often becomes a problem in separated families where Mom and Dad are struggling for *good parent* honors with their children. Each parent undermines the reinforcement of the other, only adding to the child's ultimate confusion. It is so important that parents realize the impact of the overall message they are giving their children. Like self esteem, moral behavior is not something learned in a textbook or at school on the playground. If we want our children to grow up and be decent human beings, we must work at what we ourselves are demonstrating. It is hard to ask our children to do something that we ourselves cannot model.

Words Of Caution!

Winning at any cost is a philosophy which should not apply in any sport, but in sailing, the philosophy can be deadly. Recently, it is being reported that more and more often, kids are getting high on drugs in order to relax and win their race. These young sailors actually believe that they can only win while high. Drug use has become a culture among many of these kids, and these kids reinforce each other in this behavior. It is a sorry commentary on our athletic and social system that young athletes are so stressed out playing, that they are experiencing so much pressure inside. I have discussed this with experts on both coasts, and the general feeling is that this is a relatively new phenomenon at the youth level. Besides the fact that there have been some deaths in the sailing world as a result of drugs, several competitors have found their performance beginning to suffer as discussed in the previous section of this chapter of self handicapping. People have been kicked out of regattas, out of school and out of sailing as a result of this behavior. Sailing can be deadly if safety is not always a consideration.

US SAILING makes it quite clear in the race instructions sent to every youth champion competitor that drugs will not be tolerated in any way from the time the regatta begins to the moment it ends. However, all too often, juniors are encouraged to practice on their own without any supervision or coaching away from regatta sites. Football and basketball maintains a code of performance by the coaches. Sailing is a sport usually void of such active supervised coaching.

IT IS IMPERATIVE THAT PARENTS WAKE UP AND BEGIN TO TAKE AN ACTIVE INTEREST IN THIS SUPERVISION.

1. Do not be content just letting your child go to regattas without knowing where they will stay, who they will be with, and what adults are involved.

2. Be sure to check out the coaches for their own views and values regarding performance enhancing substances. All is not necessarily what it seems to be. Do not be afraid to ask questions and to discuss with other parents your concerns.

3. Make yourself available to your child as much as possible during regattas. Make sure they have money and food and water and clothing as needed. Be there to listen if they are having doubts about what they are doing.

Sailing is a demanding sport, and it takes a toll on the competitor. Help your child become a responsible athlete by being a responsible parent.

Recreational sailing in a Laser off The Queen Mary in Long Beach.

CHAPTER 7
Sports Psychology
By
Claudia Wainer, M.A.

Claudia Wainer holds a Masters degree and is clinically trained in psychology and works with young people as a social worker for the County of Los Angeles Child Protective Services. She is also Junior Program Director at Del Rey Yacht Club in Marina Del Rey, California. Claudia has thirteen years experience working in a coaching capacity directly with junior sailors and is an accomplished one design and off shore helms person. She knows first hand how to pull together a successful campaign.

This Article is written specifically for the child from the child's point of view. If possible, let your child read this section and then work with him/her to implement the ideas. Success in sports requires as much conditioning of the mind as the body.

What Is Winning?

Everyone likes to be a *winner*. However, just to set your site on winning is not enough. Many components must come together in order to give you that winning edge. Without detail and attention given to these areas, you might as well stay ashore.

In this section, I will discuss how to organize your program, identify and set attainable goals, what it means to be mentally prepared, and how to be a Corinthian competitor. We will also explore how to deal with disappointments when a goal is not realized and how to reduce the effects of performance anxiety and *burnout*. This chapter is dedicated to the courageous junior competitor.

Organization/Eliminate Surprises:

Lack of preparation is the single most influential element which will cause you to end your sailing season prematurely. Organizing your program must begin at the onset of each racing season and is the grass roots of winning. This means that your equipment, regatta schedule, budgeting goals and expectations, and all other important travel preparation must be planned for well ahead of each regatta. Attention to all of these details will reduce surprises and help to eliminate stress which develops with last minute planning. For example, in traveling to an out of town regatta, it is better to focus mental energy on familiarization of the race course, local conditions and strategy than it is on getting housing and last minute equipment which could have been done weeks before in anticipation of the race.

Besides planning for the specifics of any one regatta, a long term assessment of the financial commitment necessary for a sailing campaign is also necessary in order for you to contact various funding sources well ahead of time to request support. If your preliminary program organization and budget can be presented as a package, it should increase your chances of receiving a commitment from your funding source.

Goal Setting:

Set realistic goals in order to maximize your confidence and minimize your disappointment. It may be more important to underestimate these goals and to later reevaluate them after frequent successes than to overstate them and contend with a lowered self confidence as a result. Here are some ways to evaluate your personal goals and motivations and maximize your confidence.

1. *Identify the reasons you are involved in your sport and specifically what personal motivation do you have for sailing.* Which of these motivations apply to you?

    A. Do you crave the competition and the thrills and chills which go along with it? *Or*
    B. Do you aspire to national/international recognition? *Or*
    C. Are you motivated by the simplicity of just being

outdoors, having the wind in your face and getting a tan at the same time? *Or*

D. Are you perfectly happy going out to race and wherever the chips fall is alright by you?

Once your personal goals and motivatons have been identified, then plan your sailing around these. If you are moderately competitive, the sailing program most appropriate for you may be quite different from a person who is highly competitive or not competitive at all. Not everyone is motivated by the same thing.

2. *Identify your long term goal for the season. What is it you ultimately want to achieve this year in this sport?* Do you want to go to the *Nautica Youth Championships* in June or the *Sears, Bemis Smythe* in August? Or, are you happy to finish in the top third of your fleet in a year end local event? Or perhaps, you may want to finish ahead of a certain other competitor in the *Nationals*? In all three of these cases, you want to highlight this goal and put the essence of your season together.

3. *Develop small short term goals to help build confidence.* Long term goals are made up of smaller short term goals which help to build confidence. This confidence is the key ingredient needed in becoming a successful competitor. Some important confidence building tasks are:

    A. Test the limits of your talents by experimenting with tactics or boat handling which you have not tried before. Stretch your skills and your abilities.

    B. Practice often to help sharpen your skills. The execution of boat handling may be the difference between rounding the leeward mark in first place or fifteenth.

    C. Expand on little successes and give yourself a pat on the back when you execute a maneuver which is successful. Be quick to recognize the strengths of your race and write what you did to get an edge on the competition. Give yourself positive feedback.

    D. Overcome your fears. Every competitor must face the fear of losing, however, much of this fear comes from being (or feeling) unprepared. This is called **performance anxiety** and can reduce performance itself. Plan ahead and work on the plan to help reduce any fear which is the result of this anxiety.

4. *As confidence builds, begin to identify areas of strength which you should expand upon and weakness which need to be improved.* For example, if my roll tacks are not as fast and smooth as they could be, I might ask my coach to drill me more in this area. If my starts are excellent and well timed, I might continue to practice them but will add more starting techniques to my arsenal so that I can begin to integrate them in practice and in races. If I take someone's stern too often and allow them to get to the favored side of the course, then I might work on becoming more aggressive and exercise my lee bow option.

In all of these examples, I have identified strengths to build upon and weaknesses to work on. These are really short term goals. If these goals are combined, I become a more competent and skilled competitor which will ultimately assist me in attaining my long term goal of competition.

Mental Preparation:

Wrapped within the experience of competition are many highs and lows. An "off day", a "God-like", day a mediocre day, or an outright "bad" day can happen to any of you. Lack of mental focus can make these hills and valleys overwhelming and even more distracting to the competitor. Maintaining your intensity of self motivation and concentration while training and competing is essential in order to execute solid tactics and boat handling. The bandits that break down this concentration are: 1). Distractions on and off the race course. 2) Stress which is caused by anxiety or worrying about your performance. 3) Pressure from outside supporters (perceived or real) such as yacht clubs and parents.

The consequence of allowing these bandits to rob your concentration, is that they slow your reflexes. The expression "sailing by the seat of your pants," refers to the experience of sailing when you are barely conscious of the decision making process that your brain is making. In close racing, you need to make split second decisions, and if not concentrating 100% on the task at hand, you may miss valuable regatta winning opportunities. Reflexes are subconscious so you must keep *airways* open between your brain and your body.

The best way to deal with the distraction, stress and pressure of racing, is to discipline yourself. You must find the **zone** which effectively blocks non-productive thinking. Like a marathon runner who must pace himself physically, a sailor's mind must conserve energy. Do not have thoughts which take you away from your main strategy. Stop thinking about parents who are watching you from the spectator boat;-they are proud of you for just being there. Stop thinking about the yacht club who supported your sailing; the members are enjoying the support of your efforts especially since you are out there representing them so competently. Your mind should be focused entirely on the race and your boat handling, and keep those non-productive thoughts away! This is what *finding the zone* is all about.

Sportsmanship:

Be a gracious and rule abiding competitor. If you find yourself consistently involved in protests, (filed by either you or someone against you) are not being a good sportsman. If you are the one who is protested in every race, then you are sailing too aggressively and not sailing smart. Even if you just "sneak in there" fairly and cleanly, your competitor may see it differently and you will find yourself in the jury room defending your fancy move. This will eventually lead to distractions in your overall sailing. Protests take a lot of time to present and to be heard. This takes valuable time away from your ability to focus on the task at hand.

A second reason to reduce your protest time is *invisibility*. Being a fast cut-up on the race course is like driving a noisy hot pink double decker bus down the road. After a short time, your competitors are going to want to blow that ugly, noisy, distracting bus out of the water. Instead, be a quiet Mercedes and just purr along. Don't draw unnecessary attention to yourself. Big gains can be made smoothly and quietly, and you will be more respected and successful on the race course as a result of it.

Don't be a sore loser! This is not part of a winning program and is very non-productive. You may believe that rude behavior is intimidating to the competition. The fact is, not only are you disrespectful when you are a sore loser, but you are also disliked. When you are pounding around on the dock telling everyone how much better you are than they are, guess how much mental energy is blowing in the wind? It's better to keep your lips zipped than to say something which will no doubt get you in big trouble. Conversely, if you come up against someone who is a poor sport, walk away...fast. Remember to remain focused and let the pink noisy double decker bus role on somewhere else.

How To Deal With A Legitimate Loss:

What if you have followed the prescription for running an organized program, assessed your skills and set your goals accordingly, and you suffer more than one disappointing finish? How do you keep going out to the race course when you apparently are not getting any better? Here are some pointers to keep your program from sinking:

1. Reframe your loss or losses and look at them as lessons to build upon. How you cope and learn from loss is critical to moving productively forward.

2. Reexamine your goals and expectations. If you are consistently performing outside your target, modify your goals so they are more aligned with your talents.

3. Do not let disappointment become self defeating. Acknowledge to yourself that all athletes go through a slump. Try to keep a positive attitude and fight having negative thoughts about your performance. In place of the word *Can't*, substitute *Will*.

4. Don't lose site of your own abilities and accomplishments. Review your strengths and weaknesses and know that it is almost impossible to forget a learned ability.

5. Work on the areas that are giving you specific problems. For example, if your leeward mark roundings are leaving you on the outside of the pack of overlapped boats, review the strategies in approaching and rounding marks in traffic, and try to apply the tactics during practice races.

How To Reduce Anxiety, Stress and Burnout:

Anxiety and Stress:

The state of being *stressed out* may be caused by mounting pressures concerning your performance, better known as **Performance Anxiety.** You may feel that you need to do well to reward your yacht club for their support or win your parent's respect. Such mental pressure may produce the following symptoms: irritability; difficulty in concentrating; sweating; nervousness; loss of appetite. These symptoms can be experienced in varying degrees and combinations. These mind and body reactions will effectively sabotage all that you have worked for and should be eliminated as much as possible.

A competitor may not be totally stress free since pressure always exists in the realm of any competitive game, however, corralling pressures and reducing stress is possible.

1. Recognize the symptoms of stress. You may experience some of these symptoms right before and during many regattas.

2. If feeling stress before a regatta, you can try the following:
    - A. Sit down quietly and review what you are stressed out about. Are you concerned about your level of practice? Your parents expectations? Your performance?
    - B. Review on paper or in your head (with your coach or parent) all of the areas you have appropriately prepared for and are now ready to execute.
    - C. Reassure yourself that you have done all of the preparation possible and that you are as ready as you can be.

3. If feeling stress during a regatta, you can try the following:
   A. Make two columns on a piece of paper. Write down all of your goals and objectives for the race in one column and your strengths in another. Place these in a water tight ziplock and tape it to a part of the boat easy to see.
   B. When stress symptoms appear, review this list. You will begin to replace negative thoughts with positive ones and your focus will return.

<u>*Burnout:*</u>

Remember when we discussed conserving mental energy? Going all out in the beginning of your campaign can lead to the syndrome called **burnout.** You will know when you are suffering from burnout when you begin to feel unmotivated and lazy and your performance on the water becomes sloppy and erratic.

You can recover from burnout by stepping back and reevaluating your goals and expectations. Lack of focus and purpose use up much needed mental energy and too much intensity lifts the pace beyond reasonable limits. Reestablish short term goals to help win back the psychological edge and appropriate pacing every competitor requires in their arsenal.

In closing, a successful campaigner has done the necessary pre season planning and has set attainable short and long term goals. Throughout the season, the competitor has reviewed and reassessed his/her own unique strengths and weaknesses and has implemented ways to maximize and minimize these areas. A competent athlete is also a good sport and is respected by peers on and off the water as well as the governing body of the class of boats they sail in. It is more important to win as a good sport as it is to win. Self confidence is such a large part of a competitor's mindset that any negative thinking or self doubt can turn the best boat handler and tactician into a back of the fleet stressed out has been. Every competitor experiences stress, but the most successful learn to deal with it. When combined with practice and skill, focus and a positive mental attitude will almost always yield exceptional results on the race course.

CHAPTER 8
Fitness For Kids
By
Chris Camacho

Chris Camacho graduated from Chapman University in 1991 with a degree in Movement/Exercise Science with an emphasis in athletic training. He is an ACE certified personal trainer and has worked with clients both in the United States and Japan for more than seven years.

In this chapter we will discuss the importance of fitness and its relationship to sailing. First, we must clarify that fitness is described as a state which characterizes the degree to which a person is able to function efficiently. Fitness is the balance between being physically healthy and emotionally sound. As parents, we may find it difficult to change lifestyles and health habits as we grow older, so the earlier we educate our children in fitness, the more likely they will carry the experience into their adult years.

When discussing physical fitness, there are three important areas which should be developed: *cardiovascular fitness, body strength, and flexibility.* All three of these are essential to the physical well being of everyone all of the time, but they become even more important when an individual decides to compete in an athletic sport such as sailing.

Cardiovascular Fitness:

Cardiovascular fitness is considered the most important aspect of the three fitness categories, and must become a vital part of any regular fitness program. By participating in regular physical exercise, the individual strengthens the heart which allows it to pump more blood per beat. A stronger heart makes the heart more efficient both during exercise and at rest. In addition, an improved cardiovascular system enables us to utilize oxygen better during such increased physical activity. A trained cardiovascular system leads to the body's ability to perform more strenuous exercise for a more sustained period of time. This increased duration allows us to work harder and gain in physical strength. Finally, although this may seem to apply more for older people than for children, cardiovascular fitness helps to lower the risk of coronary heart disease such as atherosclerosis, high blood pressure and stroke. Working with young people to develop fitness habits early, will benefit them later in life.

Muscular Strength:

Muscular strength can be defined as the total amount of force which can be exerted by a muscle with a single effort against resistance. By maintaining muscular strength, either through specific sports training or by a general exercise program, the individual can expect to benefit in several ways:

(1) They may reduce the risk of serious or mild injury by increasing the body's musculature.
(2) Increased musculature should lead to better posture thereby reducing back problems later in life.
(3) Increased muscle strength will increase endurance and provide resistance to muscular fatigue.
(4) Increased musculature may help increase the immune system's ability to fight off disease.
(5) All of this should enhance performance as a result of increased speed, strength and agility.

Flexibility:

The third and last area to develop in fitness is flexibility. Flexibility refers to the ability of a joint to have freedom of movement through its normal range of motion. By maintaining adequate flexibility, the individual will reduce the risk of orthopedic conditions such as low back pain. Flexibility is also important in certain sports specific movements and skills such as hiking out on sailboats and moving quickly from side to side of the boat during tacking maneuvers. Furthermore, flexibility decreases the chance of muscle and tendon strains and ligament sprains while lifting the heavy boats and gear.

Program Suggestions:

Four factors should be considered for any fitness program to be effective. First, the **frequency of exercise** should be on average of *three to five* times per week. Secondly, the **intensity** or effort expended, should be appropriate for the age level and skill level of each person. A program which is too strenuous, may cause injury while a program which is too light, may not provide much benefit. Next, one should consider the **duration** or length of time spent doing exercises. It has been suggested that a minimum of 40 minutes per workout session is recommended for any substantial results to occur. Finally, the **mode** of exercise or what type of equipment to use becomes a consideration in any given program. Equipment which is easy to find, such as stairs, is recommended.

Since most sailing programs meet several times per week, it is easy to add an exercise component early each day for 15-30 minutes. Forty minutes of exercise per session may take up too much program time, but, extra swimming and running during games may help add more time and diversity to the general physical fitness program. Sailors might increase the intensity of their workout depending upon how old they are and they may choose to add a variety of activities to their daily routine. The main objective in working with children is to make it seem like fun.

To enhance one's performance, whether it be in golf, running, skiing, or sailing, certain sports specific factors should be taken into consideration prior to designing a fitness program. To maximize performance in sailing for instance, it is recommended that a program consists of <u>aerobic activity</u>, <u>weight training</u> and <u>stretching.</u>

<u>Cardiovascular activity</u> such as *running* or *swimming* can be included at the beginning of almost every program day right before the daily *chalk talk*. <u>Strength</u> can be improved in the abdominal, leg and upper body arm areas using just the body and very little other equipment. This added strength will help build muscles for hiking out in heavier wind conditions and maintain endurance during longer events. It is important to remember, what may be difficult for one person, may be easy for another. There is no magical number of how much or how little exercise to do. To experience an increase in muscular strength, maximum effort is required. For those who lack the muscular strength in the beginning to perform these exercises, they may modify the exercise to enable them to be performed. Those with less strength can modify these exercises slightly to enable them be performed. Here are some exercises which are easy to do in any program to build strength.

1. Leg Strength:

A. Running up and down stairs is not only good for the legs, but it also is a great cardiovascular workout. Any set of stairs will work for this.

B. Another superb exercise for strengthening the legs is lunges. Start with both feet pointing forward and hands at your sides. Take one step out approximately 3-4 shoe lengths and bend the back knee until it almost touches the ground (your front knee will be bent as well) and then come straight back up. Return to starting position and then alternate feet. Repeat the movement.

2. Abdominal (stomach) strength:

The simplest and most effective exercise is the crunch. Begin by laying flat on your back with knees bent at an angle and feet flat on the floor. Your hands should be placed behind your head with your elbows out. Slowly crunch the abdomianls by raising your shoulders off the ground, making sure to keep your chin and nose pointed toward the ceiling. Slowly return the shoulders to the ground. Repeat this action. It is important to exhale on the upward movement and inhale on the downward movement. Continue doing this until you feel a slight burn in the abdominals. Rest for 15-30 seconds and repeat the exercise again.

3. Upper Body Strength:

For the upper body there are two exercises which can improve one's muscular strength as well as endurance. Each exercise uses the individual's own body weight as resistance.

A. <u>Military push-ups increase the strength of the pectorals (chest), deltoids (shoulders) and triceps (back of arm).</u>

To perform these push-ups, the individual should start on a surface free of any foreign objects. Lay flat on the stomach with the hands placed slightly wider than shoulder width. Keeping the back flat, have the individual push their body weight upwards. Do not fully lock the elbows at the top of the motion. Slowly, descend to the point where the elbows are bent at a 90 degree angle and then drive the body upwards once again. The exercise may be modified by placing the knees on the ground. This is to enable those who lack upper body strength to perform the exercise.

B. <u>Military pull-ups work the latissimus dorsi (back) and biceps (front of arm).</u>

There are two basic grips that are used while performing pull-ups. The overhand (palms facing away from the body) and the underhand (palms facing towards the body). Alternating the grip may produce the best results. The bar should be high enough to allow the individual to hang freely when the knees are bent. Hands should be shoulder width apart. Slowly, pull the body upward to the point where the chin is above the bar, then slowly descend to the starting position and repeat the motion.

I recommend starting with two sets of each exercise. Try to do as many repetitions as possible, and progressively increase the set number to three while still performing the maximum repetitions the body can do without becoming too fatigued.

Finally, to maximize flexibility and minimize the potential for injury, it is important to stretch before and after a physical workout. The following stretches are recommended:
1. *Back and Hamstring Stretch:*
While lying on your back, pull one leg towards your chest and hold. Keep the opposite leg as straight as possible. Lower the leg and repeat the motion with the other leg.

2. *Quadriceps:*
While standing, bend one knee and place the heel of that foot at the base of the buttocks. Hold the top of the one foot with the opposite hand and gently pull your foot toward your buttock. Perform this action on both legs.

There are several important factors to remember while stretching. 1) Maintain normal breathing throughout the stretch. 2) Hold each stretch for twenty to thirty seconds. 3) Do not bounce or jerk while stretching. The motion should be controlled and gradual.

Sports Injuries:
As with every physical activity, there is always a chance of injury. The best way of avoiding a sports injury is by using preventive techniques. Although sailing is considered to be a non-contact sport (between people), injuries may still happen. Among the less serious of these are the traditional bumps, scrapes, and bruises which occur to everyone no matter how experienced. Small children tend to get their fingers pinched in their tiller extensions or more seriously, get their hands squashed between their boat and the dock as they reach to stop a boat. Heads are sometimes bumped by the boom as it swings from side to side. And finally, toes are stubbed while getting in and out of the boat. Most of these injuries hurt, but they are not serious and can be treated with a few bandaids and *TLC* (tender loving care).

However, there are some sports injuries which are far more critical. It has been shown in research studies, that the highest incident of sports deaths come from **heatstroke**. While this may not seem possible on the water of cooler harbors such as on the west or northwest coasts, the southern harbors often find temperatures climbing to 90 degrees or higher with an 80% humidity level making four hours of sailing quite uncomfortable for almost anyone. Dehydration, lack of food and fatigue may all combine to increase the chances for serious injury and poor performance. For this reason, it is imperative for all sailors, especially young ones, to bring along water bottles and to constantly hydrate themselves. Water bottles can be secured in just about any boat, and parents should insist upon them as much as sunscreen, sunglasses and hats. In addition to water, on longer sailing days, quick energy food should be brought along to keep the blood sugar levels high. Plastic sacks can be filled with a child's favorite healthy snack. You might watch out for soft foods which will only get squished in the bottom of the boat.

As with any athletic activity, it is important to have a first aid kit available for emergencies. The following items are recommended:
1. Adhesive bandages (small and large sizes)
2. Antiseptic (for burns, stings, bites and rashes)
3. Ammonia Capsules (smelling salts) - Not to be used if any indication of a neck injury since it may cause a violent

    head jerk which could cause more spinal injury.
4. Aspirin/non-aspirin
5. Elastic wraps (ace Bandages)
6. Instant ice packs
7. Gauze pads
8. Adhesive tape
9. Any medication the child may need (asthma, antibiotics, etc.) should be given to the program director at the beginning of the day with a note of authorization and how to use it.
10. If in an earthquake zone, enough food and water for three days for each child as well as blankets, battery operated radio and flashlights.

Conclusion:

In order to maximize one's ability to compete, a fitness program must be in place several weeks before the actual event. It is not enough to work out one or two weeks prior to a regatta and think that any major good will come from it. It takes at least three or four weeks, or more, of solid preparation to be in top form. So it is important to plan ahead for competition (**see Chapter 7 Sports Psychology**) and physical fitness should be considered part of that planning schedule.

Finally, fitness does not just mean working out for hours each program day. Total fitness should become a lifestyle. Children can be taught that a proper diet (low in unsaturated fats), exercise and adequate rest is essential to one's total health. But true fitness is more than just being physically fit with exercise and diet. It is also being emotionally sound. Probably the most important factor of an overall fitness program is to enjoy the activity in which you are engaged in. People will only participate in an activity if it is enjoyable, so any fitness program must by fun. Children as well as adults need variety in their day in order to keep focused. A varied program of recreation and physical fitness can be part of a total fitness program which can be enjoyed for years to come.

CHAPTER 9
An Instructor's View

The typical sailing instructor has come up through the ranks of being a junior sailor for many summers. Although some instructors may be in their 20s or 30s and bring with them a wealth of education experience, most are considerably younger with practical on the water experience. but far less classroom based experience. Program curriculums vary by location, so parents should check out all of the program quality issues which have been discussed in **Chapter 2**. It is my editorial opinion, although biased as it may seem, that parents need to remind themselves that sailing is a voluntary recreational activity, conducted in organized programs throughout the country, but it is not mandatory school. Instructors are trained for perhaps many years, but they are not professional educators. They are hired to teach a loved skill and are not paid to baby-sit children.

An important contribution a parent can make to their child's sailing education, is to visit the program and see for him/herself just what a typical day is like. For example, one summer we had a child who just refused to put sunscreen on his face even though all of the instructors and the life guard reminded him. When that child received a bad sunburn, the parents were furious with the staff and threatened to pull the child from the program. I remember talking with the staff and it was determined that the child would require a one to one instructor-student ratio in order to effectively solve the problem. Although this was a serious problem for the family, the parents were advised that greater personal responsibility was mandatory. The staff was alerted to keep reminding the child to put on the sunscreen, but it was expected that the parents would make sure that it was applied at home before he came to the program.

During another summer, a child found herself miserable because she felt that everyone but she could rig and unrig their boat independently by the end of the second day. Both of the parents were upset because the staff seemed to ignore her individual needs (based on their daughter interpretation). Yet, after some investigation, it was determined that the young girl was brand new to the program and indeed some of the students were more skilled in rigging then she was. Further, on the second day of her session, she left early for a doctor's appointment making it difficult for the staff to take her aside individually. Her parents had asked her to unrig her boat before she was picked up, but because everyone was busy attending to the regular program, she was unable to get the special help required to unrig her boat and put it away. Since she missed some of the important experiences that day, she and her parents were upset on returning and finding her boat moved by the instructors to make room for other kids. They could not understand why a staff member was not available to give special consideration to their child. Parents need to remember that a program is staffed with one instructor per 5-8 kids. Any special considerations should become the parent's responsibility if for no other reason then the fact that staff is attending to many things at once on and off the water. To help you understand what a typical program day and instructor is like, I have included the following interview.

Jason Artof is an instructor at Del Rey Yacht Club in Marina Del Rey where he has taught sailing for several years. His background and experience qualifies him as a good representative of what an average sailing instructor is like throughout the country. He has won some major championship regattas including the US *SAILING/ROLEX Junior Championships* in 1989 (doublehanded with Peter Wells), The *US SAILING Singlehanded Championship* semi finals and the *US SAILING/ROLEX Junior Championship* (singlehanded) semi finals in 1992 and the Capri 14.2 Nationals in 1992 and 1993. He has also been selected to sail in the *NAUTICA/US SAILING Youth Championships* sailed in Gulfport, Mississippi; Milwaukee Wisconsin; Alamitos Bay, California; and Greenwich, Connecticut as well as selected as part of the *Los Angeles Youth*

Sailing Team which participated in Nagoya Japan in 1989. At this time, Jason is completing his second year of college at University of California Irvine and is a Mechanical Engineering major and a member of the UCI Varsity Sailing Team. Sailing has been an important part of his life, even helping him to focus on a career path in engineering.

1. **How long have you been sailing?**

I began sailing when I was 7 1/2 years old. I wanted to begin the program, but I admit that it scared me for a few seasons. I needed to get used to the wind and what that did to the boat.

2. **How long have you been an instructor?**

I became an instructor's assistant when I was in 10th grade. I must have been 15 years old at the time. I didn't want to stop taking sailing classes, but I also wanted to work and had taken enough sailing clinics from other instructors to know something about teaching. The next year I was an instructor and remained one for two seasons. I was made Head Instructor last year, after my first year of college.

3. **What kind of training did you need to become Head Instructor of a major program?**

To become an instructor in my program it is mandatory to take an instructor training class, and the best class available is the US SAILING Instructor training. I became Level 1 certified. This year I am trying to find a Level 2 class which meets my schedule. I have also taken three years of CISA (California International Sailing Association) seminars which offer some of the best teaching from some of the best teachers around. There are Olympians and coaches from all over that participate in this training. Finally, since I have been traveling all around the country in the US SAILING Championships, I have been fortunate to participate in seminars offered for each regatta. All of this training has helped me understand what is good and bad teaching. I remember being a kid and the fear I felt trying to master the boat. I hope I can help others get over that fear.

4. What does a typical day look like to you during the summer program?

Our program runs 4 days per week (Mon.-Thurs.) and begins a 8:45 AM and ends at 4:00 PM. Kids come early in the morning and take about an hour to rig their boats. Since it is summer, some kids straggle in a little later and we tell everyone to meet on the patio near the pool at 9:45 AM for what we call a chalk talk or instruction using the black board.

At this chalk talk, everyone warms up with some sort of exercise and perhaps a few laps around the clubhouse. Many of the kids grumble about this and try to convince the instructors that this is not a PE class, but I feel that it is important to strengthen and condition the body even during the summer. After the exercises, we usually break into skill level groups with beginners, intermediates and advanced sailors breaking off with a different instructor. Sometimes the entire group will be doing the same thing such as sailing to the park or working on a relay race or sailing project, and groups will not be formed. If groups are formed, then each instructor will discuss a new point of sailing with their students during individual chalk talks after the main one.

Kids will then go out on their boats and work on certain drills or sail to a part of the harbor for some fun and recreation. We always have two chase boats available and are working on getting a third so that each group can actually sail in a different place of the harbor. During the last few summers, we must combine the beginning and intermediate groups more often than I would like.

Everyone sails until approximately 12:00-12:30 and we then sail back for lunch. Some of the kids buy their lunch and some bring it. We relax and eat. After digesting, we break into groups again with the better sailors going back out to sail and race for the next two hours while the less skilled sailors go to the swimming pool to work on conditioning and swimming skills. At approximately 2:30-3:00 everyone sails back to unrig their boats and finish the day swimming.

A few times per week, students can remain until 7:00-8:00 PM and race in evening races which are sponsored by different yacht clubs in the harbor. Parents are encouraged to come and support their kids during these late afternoon races.

5. What is the biggest problem you have had to encounter as an instructor?

Of course I've had the scary problems of kids getting knocked on the head with their booms or cuts on their fingers. We have first aid kits around, and our life guard is always available. All of the instructors are trained in CPR and First Aid and we have a full-time staff person in the office to call paramedics for any emergencies. Fortunately, we have never had a major incident, but we try to be alert all of the time.

The worst problems we have are behavioral. Sometimes kids come to the program and are just rebelling about doing anything. These kids can sit around and complain all day no matter what we have them doing. This makes it bad for the other kids who really want to be there. If kids do not want to come to a volunteer program, then maybe they shouldn't. Once kids get bored, the instructors can never get them back for that day. It is just better to keep everyone busy and not let them get bored. It is hard keeping this energy up all day if kids begin to complain.

Other problems we seem to have are kids teasing other kids. Since everyone is around water all day, sometimes the teasing can get out of hand. Our instructors need to keep alert all of the time to enforce standards. If we forget to communicate these standards the kids seem to push the limits more and more. It is important for parents to help their kids understand that sailing is a volunteer activity and that there are certain rules which should be followed or else the child will be asked to leave.

I will also admit that I have had some problems with other instructors. When I ask them to do something and they don't do it, I have to talk with the parents about it or even my own Director. I can't be everywhere at once. Last summer I had some problems with a staff member who was more difficult to discipline then the kids. Obviously, we are not reemploying that person this summer.

6. **What is it like to work with brand new beginning sailors. Can you relate to them?**

I like working with new kids if they are enthusiastic. I know that they are frightened of new things, but enthusiasm is contagious and makes it fun for everyone. In our program we give nicknames to some of the kids, and we look forward to these kids coming to class. Even if they have a hard time learning how to sail, they will be the best one's later. Probably the worst thing about working with beginners is when they are too young to really become part of the group and they just cannot understand what is going on.

7. **What is the most important quality an instructor should have on order to work with beginning sailors?**

Patience! It takes a lot of patience to work with kids and help them have fun. A good instructor does not have to be the best racer, but they have to be able to work well with kids and keep them enthusiastic.

8. **How do you handle discipline problems? What is a common technique you make use of?**

We have problems every year with kids who push limits of everyone's patience. We have developed a code of standards which kids and their parents must sign before coming to the program. This list includes rules for where the kids can go while in the program, how they should act with others and so forth. However, this year we had more problems with stealing, bad language and general disrespect towards both instructors and other kids. We developed an even stricter set of standards to sign and each parent is informed that the child will be sent home if these rules are violated. It seems simple, but some parents were not aware that their children were causing any problems, so we are informing them early about any such concerns.

The smaller problems are usually handled by taking the student out of the class and asking them to have a time out with the life guard. Usually this works, although, sometimes the child likes sitting at the pool more than sailing and they begin to find ways to get in trouble. We also have kids helping to clean up and do work or extra exercises when they have a bad day. We must be flexible since everyday is different. There is always a challenge.

One thing we definitely do not do is use any form of physical punishment with the child.

9. How do you handle fear in young kids?

I was afraid of sailing when I was young, and I know that the best way of handling fear is to encourage the child. Sometimes having an older sailor work with a younger one helps. Sometimes taking the child out of the group and working solo with them works.

Positive feedback works well with fearful kids. If they are worried about the wind blowing, get their minds onto something else and encourage them into getting into the boat. When they see that other people are having fun, they may get their courage up and try to overcome the fear. In our program we also have everyone practice capsizing their boats so they can actually experience the worst thing that can happen. The more they do that, the less fear they will have. They gain more control.

What doesn't work is yelling or embarrassing the child. We don't do that in our program and neither should parents.

10. What tips can you give parents to help their kids in a sport such as sailing?

As I was saying about fear, yelling and humiliating the child is not right. Kids have feelings, and parents should not make them feel badly. Parents have to realize that sailing is difficult even though it may look easy. I suggest that parents get on the small boats with their children and see what it is like. In our program we have a race which encourages this. It is called the junior senior race, and kids sail a relay type race with their parents. The winning team is one where both the young sailor and the beginning parent sailor actually completes the race course. Kids have a chance to yell out encouragement to their parents.

Another tip I can give is to encourage parents to be at the races when their kids are competing. Not everyone wins, and having a parent there makes you feel good when you have had a bad day. Besides, if you do win, it feels really good to have a parent there to greet you at the dock. In our program, we make a party out of race day, and we bring over kids to act as a rooting section even if they are not racing. Parents are then encouraged to come back to the clubhouse for a bar-b-que. This has become a tradition, and kids can unrig their boats with their parents there to help. Get involved.

Also, sometimes winning championships at too young an age can be hard on a kid. Their expectations are too high and they feel that they are under a lot of pressure to perform. Be careful about pushing your child too hard and too soon.

11. What tips can you give a kid to help them develop their skills?

Have fun! If you don't have fun, why do it? Practice and don't get discouraged. Get your friends to sail with you. It is not fun to sail alone, and if your friends sail, it feels like summer all of the time. You can only get better if you practice. Also, keep your body physically fit. Races are lost because people get tired. Drink lots of water and take a snack out for long races. Keep your head clear and focused.

12. Finally, you have traveled the country in competitive sailing. What has sailing really given to you? How has it influenced your life?

Well, it has given me an outlet and a chance to be competitive so when things didn't go well in one area of my life, I could turn to sailing. It made me feel better about myself as I grew up. It has given me a good tan -yes I wear sunscreen- and something to do each summer since I was 7 1/2 years old. Sailing has sculpted my mind and helped me think about things in a different way. I ask a lot of questions about how things work. You might say that I think of things in an engineering sort of way and I did this a long time before I decided to become an engineer. I have always thought of things in a large scale sort of way, like asking questions about the clouds and the weather and how all of this will effect my performance.

At one point of my life I was going to design boats. Fast boats. Now that I'm an engineering student at UCI, a lot of the *projects I am doing in my classwork are on sailing. When I was in high school I remember doing a semester term project on sailing. My teachers did not know how to sail, so they were very impressed without really knowing what I was talking about.*

I've been able to travel a lot with my sailing, and I always have something to do when I get there. I like to be active. Anywhere there is water there are boats. I like to travel near water.

Sailing has probably helped me get into the college of my choice since I am on a varsity sailing team. My resume looked good when I applied and even though there is no money in sailing, the university supports its sailors with extra help getting classes, extra tutorial services and extra guidance counseling which has been a great help to me.

CHAPTER 10
A View From A Junior
By
Lindsay Artof

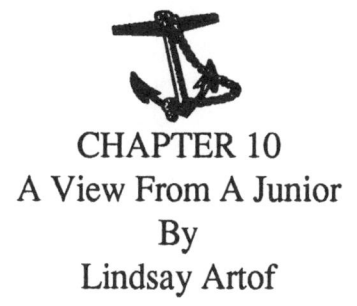

Hey, I'm Lindsay and this is my chapter to let you know everything about what is like to be in a junior sailing program. I've been in the junior program at Del Rey Yacht Club for about 10 years, so I should be able to do this. I began sailing about 15 years ago and began the program when I was 5 years old.

In the program, I've always been known as "Jason's little sis," "the instructor's sister," or the "coordinator's daughter." I have not been known for just me and my sailing. However, about 4 years ago my family moved to Westlake Village and I began to sail on Westlake Lake last year. Since I've moved, many people I've met don't know that I have a national champion sailor for a brother, so I've actually earned my own recognition by myself. I think that it is important that I've learned to do this, since at this point of my life, I've been winning more races than ever before.

Enough background about me, now let's get back to the program. In the past 10 years, I've had a blast every summer as well as during the rest of the sailing season (which in California is all year long). I've made some good friends as well as some bad ones; and I had good times and some bad ones. For example, a few years ago I seemed to "max" my potential in Sabots since I was always ahead of my fleet during the program practices. The instructors (especially my brother) began to push me harder and harder in the program until I began to dread going. Then my brother explained to me that it was important to keep improving my skills and the only way to do that was to work harder then anyone else in the program. I felt better, but still didn't like being pushed harder than anyone else. I have to admit though, I do get jealous when someone is better than me. But, I have to deal with this. Personally, I sail somewhat for the feeling of competition but basically for the *fun* (Jason, if you're reading this, that's my answer for everytime you ask me what I want to do with sailing).

The program has been so much a part of me for so long, that this year I have to make some hard choices. I'm going to go to summer school but I also want to teach. Even though Westlake Yacht Club is a closer program to where I live and where I am going to summer school, I have been thinking about all of the past programs at Del Rey Yacht Club, and I just can't let that go. Last summer I also went to summer school, but my Mom drove me after school into Marina Del Rey (35 miles) each day which took about an hour. I volunteered to help with the beginning kids from 1:00 PM until 7-8:00 PM several nights per week. I don't know if I would like to work for free again this year, but I probably would just to be there because I have so many good memories of my summers. I just cannot let that go. It's my life. I would miss sailing over to the "park" and playing "capture the flag" with everyone, even the instructors. I would miss going to "Baskin Robins 31 Flavors" for ice cream and then there were the "scavenger hunts" where we sailed around the marina using clues to look for hidden objects. Finally, I would miss going to "Fisherman's Village" once per session for lunch and shopping.

The junior sailing program has been great for me because it separates me from other people who do sports like soccer, softball and basketball. As far as I am concerned, I'm original, and that's the way I'm going to stay! I hope to see more kids out on the water. Bye at least for now. Who knows, maybe I'll be asked to write another chapter in another book.

CHAPTER 11
Sailing Organizations

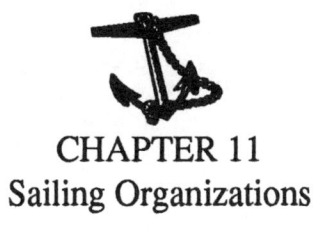

Sometimes called the alphabet soup, the organizational map of United States sailing moves from the national level of organizations to the local region, each with its own alphabet description of labels. Because I am from Southern California, I will discuss these labels as they apply to our specific region, but there are regions for each specific area of the country which will apply directly to you, the reader.

National Organization:
The *National Governing* body for sailing in the United States is called **The United States Sailing Association (US SAILING)**. The basic function of **US SAILING** is to administer racing, education and training programs for all sailors and sailing instructors, develop and administer race officer recognition programs, and conduct certain **US SAILING** Championships. Except for a small paid staff which is located in Newport Rhode Island, **US SAILING** is run by volunteers who have developed an exceptional love for the sport. They are willing to devote much of their time and money to help administer the many programs this organization has become famous for including most of the safety and race management programs which affect our youth.

US SAILING is divided into ten *Areas* or *Councils* which are broken into *Yacht Racing Associations* (YRAs). Each Area is designated by a letter of the alphabet (see the map on page 108 for area boundaries). Letters A-H and J and K represent each of these areas. *Area Directors* are selected for each area and serve on a *Council of Sailing Associations* (CSA) All Areas have regular Council meetings where important matters of the specific region are discussed including the specifics for **US SAILING** ladder events. The *Area Directors* are asked to be on the **US SAILING** *Association's Board of*

Directors and they attend meetings (especially the annual **US SAILING** meeting held each year in October) to discuss the direction American sailing is going. For example, the Area J Council (the Area I sail out of) Director will report all of our regional concerns at that meeting. This type of regional direction makes sailing one of the most democratically run sports in America.. In addition to the Council of Sailing Associations, there is a One Design Council, a National Offshore Council, a Multihull Council, an Industry Advisory Board and a Community Sailing Council.

US SAILING "AREAS"

As described in the **US SAILING** 1993 Directory

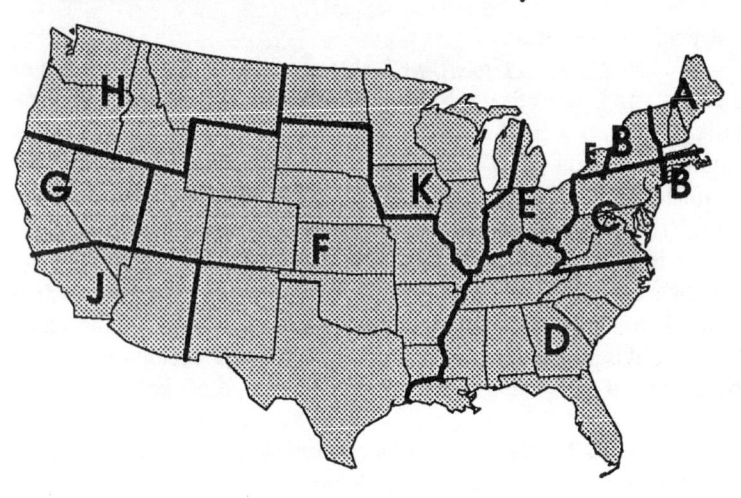

US SAILING COUNCILS

As described in the **US SAILING** 1993 directory

Area A
Maine YRA
Narragansett Bay YRA
Southern Mass YRA
YRU of Massachusetts Bay

Area B
Central New York YRA
Eastern Conn. SA
Eastern LIYA
Great South Bay YRA
YRA of LI Sound
Hudson River YRA

Area C
Barnegat Bay YRA
Chesapeake Bay YRA
Mid-Atlantic YRA
North Jersey YRA

Area D
Dixie Inland YRA
Florida SA
Gulf YA
South Atlantic YRA

Area E
Detroit Regional YA
Inter-Lake YA
Lake Huron YA
Lake YRA
Ohio Inter-Club YA

Area F
Central States SA
SA of Intermountain Lakes
Texas SA

Area G
SBRA of Northern California
YRA of SF Bay

Area H
Hawaii YRA
Pacific International YA

Area J
Southern Calif. YA
YRA of Southern Calif.

Area K
Inland Lake YA
Lake Michigan SRF
Lake Superior YA
Midwest SA
North Central SA

Besides the specific Councils which make up the main structure of **US SAILING**, the organization is broken into several committees including special committees for Olympic Yachting Race Administration, Inshore and Offshore Sailing, General Services, and Training. There are even special committees devoted to sailors with special needs, legal and government concerns, and international yachting all working through **US SAILING**. In addition, **US SAILING** helps to select the official US Olympic Sailing Team members. Thus, any changes in the racing rules, safety at sea programs or even new developments in instructor certification, are all coordinated through this highly visible national organization

To sail in any of the **US SAILING** Championship regattas, or to even attend many of the programs or to be on any of the special committees, a person must be a member of the organization. Membership costs in 1993 were as follows:
    $12 Youth (U.S. resident under 21)
    $50 Family, Contributing or Non U.S. resident
    $35 Renewing Member (single and over 21)
    $35 New Member (U.S. resident)
Because **US SAILING** has contributed so much to the sport, the organization encourages sailors to become involved early in their introduction to the sport. Everyone wins when the participants of the sport act to support it. Junior sailors are encouraged to join as either an individual youth member or as a family member. **US SAILING** has also initiated a special *Junior Golden Anchor* program aimed at youth organizations, scholastic and collegiate teams and clubs, community sailing programs and junior yacht clubs. As described in the *1993 US SAILING Directory,* "a group need only pledge to sign up 100% of the youth sailors in their group" and they may qualify to establish a Junior Golden Anchor Program. In 1993, membership dues were $7.50 compared to the $12 for unaffiliated juniors. Coaches, faculty advisors, parents and even local merchants can support junior sailing by joining **US SAILING** at the *Golden Anchor (for adults)* reduced rate of $25 compared to $35 when unaffiliated. At present,

Youth membership in all classes accounts for 22.2% of total **US SAILING** membership. A sport is only as good as the participants in it, and the philosophy of encouraging responsibility in our junior sailing participants seems to be working quite well. These kids seem to be developing a good attitude about the sport they have chosen.

In addition to the genuine help in running most of the important sailing activities in the United States, **US SAILING** also publishes a magazine called *American Sailor* which reports on all of the latest information in the national sailing world. Articles are included on collegiate and junior sailing, race management, interpretation of racing rules, as well as the latest legislative developments. Beginning in 1994, the organization has affiliated with *Sailing World Magazine* and is offering a free subscription to the magazine as part of the membership package. For a young sailor and their family, both of these magazines are terrific ways of keeping involved with the sport

Finally, for information regarding ways to fund a specific program, campaign, or ways to develop training or special community based programs in your area, you might want to contract **US SAILING FOUNDATION (USSF)**. This organization has dispensed more than $2,500,00 in grants and is the motor behind the U.S. Sailing Team as well as development of sportsmanship values such as the **US SAILING** Rescue Medal. Another way a person might get involved in the sailing world without putting in much time, is to consider calling USSF and offer a donation for their endowment fund. USSF is a tax-free, non profit organization recognized by the IRS under 501(c)(3) and donations could qualify as a tax deduction for the donor to the extent permitted by law. Talk this over with your tax advisor.

For more information about **US SAILING** and its programs, contact:

US SAILING
P.O. Box 209
Newport, RI 02840
or call (401) 849-5200

Area Organization:
As mentioned above, **US SAILING** is comprised of 10 *Areas*, each headed by its own director who reports to the national Board of Directors. Our family lives in Southern California and sails in what is called **Area J**. If we lived in Florida, we would be part of **Area D** and if we sailed out of San Francisco (Northern California) we would be a part of **Area G** (See Pg. 108-109 for Areas). Each area is then divided into local harbor regions made up of individual yacht clubs located in that particular area. These local areas are called *Associations*. I sail out of Del Rey Yacht Club (**DRYC**) which is located in Marina Del Rey and is part of an Association of yacht clubs called <u>*The Association Of Santa Monica Bay Yacht Clubs*</u> (**ASMBYC**). I am also a member of Westlake Yacht Club (**WIYC**) located on a lake within the Santa Barbara and Ventura harbors and a part of <u>*The Association Of Santa Barbara Channel Yacht Clubs*</u> (**ASBCYC**).

Each local Association may have its own ladder elimination races to determine champion level competitors who will continue on to the **US SAILING** Championships. These Association winners will then compete in Area elimination races, the winner going to the final national level championship. For example, there is a youth event sailed each year to determine the best singlehanded, doublehanded and multiple crewed boat champions. This regatta is called the *US SAILING/ROLEX JUNIOR CHAMPIONSHIP,* and competitors sail to win either the *Smythe Trophy* for Singlehanded sailors, the *Bemis Trophy* for doublehanded sailors or the *Sears Trophy* for Multiple handed crew Trophy. In Area J there are five separate harbor associations. **ASMBYC** and **ASBCYC** are two of those five. Our son Jason competed for the doublehanded *Bemis Trophy* back in 1989 and won the local harbor elimination, making him eligible to sail for the Area J elimination. He and his partner, Peter Wells, also won that regatta and were then sent back to Greenwich, Connecticut where they sailed the finals at Indian Harbor Yacht Club (**IHYC**). They won that regatta and were award the US *SAILING/ROLEX JUNIOR CHAMPIONSHIP* for doublehanded sailing and were the winners of the *Bemis Trophy*. A few years later Jason won the **Area J** elimination's for the *Smythe Trophy* and the *O'Day Trophy* leading to the *US Singlehanded Sailing Championship* and went to the **US SAILING** Finals for both. Besides conducting the elimination level races for these championships, local Harbor Associations often support junior sailing by offering extra training/coaching as well as funding for many of the young competitors who are working so hard to succeed at their sport.

Yacht Club Organization:

A person is not required to be affiliated with a yacht club or Harbor Association in order to sail. But, sailing/yacht clubs do offer something special to the general boating community. Boating might be considered a lifestyle which encourages friendly cooperation and sportsmanship among its participants, and boaters who meet other boaters may become instant friends. Yacht clubs help to form a common interest bond between people adding to the quality of social and educational activities. There are well over 2,000 such clubs spread across the United States, and several thousand other clubs throughout the world. Some of these organizations maintain a roster of only a few members and no actual clubhouse facility. Members only get together for an occasional meeting at a local restaurant and all other functions are on member's boats. Dues may be as little as $25 per year for such a club. Then there are other yacht clubs which are far more elaborate in their facilities and may offer swimming pools and restaurants as well as gas docks, local anchorage and immediate help when needed while cruising. These clubs may hire staff including club managers and dock captains along with full time junior activity directors. But, however different in staff and facility availability a club is, most clubs belonging to a Harbor Association, such as **ASMBYC,** will be involved with yachting and boating activities and offer help in race management and safety education along with a full calendar of racing and social events. Some clubs even offer reciprocal privileges to members of other clubs so that these members might travel throughout the world and find a gracious welcome mat laid out for them.

YRUs (Yacht Racing Organizations):
Individual yacht clubs within each harbor are connected by regional yachting associations also called **YRUs** or **yacht racing unions** though most of the boats participating in any major regatta are usually too small to be considered *yachts*. Southern California has two different YRUs governing the area. **Del Rey Yacht Club** and **Westlake Yacht Club** are both a part of one such organization called The *Southern California Yachting Association* **(SCYA)** which conducts its own regatta (Midwinters), holds meetings where yacht club delegates discuss problems, and administers training seminars on race management and Safety at Sea. Another club organization or Yacht Racing Union connects clubs together which have specific facilities such as dining rooms and junior programs and which are considered to be nonprofit, that is, owned and operated by the members rather than for a profit centered corporation. **YRUSC** is the Southern California chapter of this organization and conducts club management programs where clubs can share their successes and discuss management problems and other issues related to the overall boating community.

These YRU organizations also help to support various boater lobbying organizations which may influence Federal and State laws affecting all boaters. For example, recently there was a successful effort to help overturn a Federal Boat User Tax on vessels over 15 feet. There is also an effort to forestall a recent Coast Guard requirement which will make it mandatory that sailing instructors, even those on small lakes, pass and be licensed to operate large for hire passenger boats, something which will instantly dissolve most of the community and club sailing programs in our country. Running a 15 ft. chase boat is not the same as operating a 100 ft. charter boat, but the licensing requirements are being interpreted the same.

Finally, there are groups which have formed to assist the YRUs in developing certain mission statements. One special such group in California is called the *Southern California Youth Yacht Racing Association* **(SCYYRA)** and works directly with SCYA to develop and enrich youth sailing programs in the Southern California area. This organization sponsors a number of junior regattas, identifies potential champion sailors, and works with **US SAILING** to improve the quality of junior programs throughout the region. Other such youth organizations are in full operation throughout various regions of the country. Get in touch with your local association and find out how you might become more involved in your region.

SCYYRA also co-sponsors a special clinic called the **CISA** clinic held each year at Alamitos Bay Yacht Club in California. **CISA** *(California International Sailing Organization)* was established in 1971 as a non profit group whose mission is to help identify and develop the talents of youth sailors throughout the country. The organization raises money for Olympic bound competitors and trains Olympic hopefuls. In 1993 over 90 sailors from 11 states and Canada participated in the clinic by sailing Lasers, Laser IIs and Club Flying Juniors. They were treated to land and sea instruction by some of the world's best talents all brought together for this one special week during Spring Break. This clinic is open to all young sailors (most 16 years of age or older) who are selected by resume. Contact CISA in early winter for an application and information (address is at the end of this chapter).

So, now you have an overview of the alphabet soup organizations which keeps the motor driving in this sport called sailing. There is an interesting tradition which goes along with the yachting community. Every year, at a prearranged time in the spring, yacht clubs around the country celebrate the beginning of the yachting season in a ceremony called *Opening Day*. On this day, members and their families along with delegates from many of the local and regional boating organizations, get together wearing their prescribed uniforms, shoot off small canons or shotguns, raise *burgees* (yacht club flags), recite prayers of thanks for a chance to participate in this unique recreational sport, and then eat themselves silly. On the east coast and in the midwestern lake regions, the yachting season is only a few months long, with ice and snow affecting all but the heartiest ice sailors in the winter. On the west coast and in the south, sailors delight in their sport all year around. But everyone agrees, "There is nothing - absolutely nothing - half so much doing, as simply messing about in boats...or with boats...In or out of 'em, it doesn't matter." *Kenneth Grahame, The Wind in the Willows* (1908). And why not begin when you are young.

Special championship regattas designed especially for juniors are included below. There are some very specific eligibility rules for these races, so be sure to check with **US SAILING** to determine if the criterion for sailing is in fact established.

Junior Match Racing Championships:
    Governors Cup Match Race: A three person Team from each club whose members have reached their 15th birthday by the first day of racing and have not yet reached 20 years of age. The race is sailed in Santana 20 boats (or whatever the host club Balboa Yacht Club chooses).

There are a limited number of slots for this race and teams are selected by resume. Send resume to request a team entry to Balboa Yacht Club.

US SAILING Championships:
    NAUTICA/US SAILING Youth Championships
    (Youth Champs)

Applicants must be members of **US SAILING** and cannot have reached their 20th birthday in the year of the race. Participants are chosen by resume for the best singlehanded, doublehanded and board sailors in the United States. Approximately 150 youths participate in this race which is held at a different yacht club each year. There are a limited number of charter boats available, so early filing of charter requests is important once you are accepted. Often times individual clubs will help defray the cost of transportation to this regatta for the sailor, although parents and family costs must be paid for individually. Housing arrangements are included in the cost of this regatta as well as food and entertainment. There is a **US SAILING CLINIC** attached to all of the high level championship races which make just participating in these regattas something of an experience which cannot be duplicated. This event is usually sailed the third week of June and participants remain in the area for close to one week. The winners of each class who are under 19 years of age are selected for the Team Nautica which participates in the Youth World Championships later in the season.

US SAILING/ROLEX Junior Championships
Sears Cup/Bemis and Smythe Trophies

Unlike the Youth Champs, this race is for participants aged 13-18 who are members of **US SAILING** and all crew must be from the same yacht club or community sailing organization of a club recognized by the local YRA. The Sears Cup is sailed in a 3-4 person boat; The Bemis Trophy is sailed in a 2 person boat; The Smythe Trophy is sailed in a one person boat. Competitors qualify through ladder events organized by harbor associations and **US SAILING** areas. Contact **US SAILING** (401) 849-5200 for the name and number of your local ladder event organizer. Like the Youth Champs, this event is sailed at a different yacht clubs each year. Parents are invited to watch this event on provided spectator boats. The event is usually sailed during the third week of August and participants remain in the area for close to a week including the pre-race clinic. All boats are provided for. Housing and food arrangements are made for each child to stay with a family and these arrangements are mandatory. No child is allowed to be housed with their parent for this event. Area winners who are eligible for the finals are usually able to secure funding from their home club, Association, and/or Area so be sure to ask.

US SAILING/ROLEX Junior Women's Championship
Nancy Leiter Clagett Trophy

An open event for women under 19 years of age who are members of **US SAILING** and sailed in singlehanded boats (usually radial rigged lasers). Participation is by resume and application. This race is sailed in clubs throughout the United States and is sailed usually the beginning weeks of August. Ask about funding through your club and Association. Some charter boats are available if applied for early, but the best boats are usually brought from home. Parents are encouraged to participate on spectator boats if arrangements are made. Housing arrangements are made for each participant in case parents do not come.

US SAILING/ROLEX Junior Windsurfing Championship
Massachusetts Bay Trophy/IMCO National Championship
Competitors must not yet turn 19 by the first day of the event. This is an open championship sailed in Mistral IMCO boards. All windsurfing enthusiasts who are members of **US SAILING** are invited to apply. Housing and food arrangements are made for each sailor participating Boards are provided for the regatta. Funding may be available so make sure to ask about sources.

US SAILING Singlehanded Championships
O'Day Trophy
Open to **US SAILING** members 16 years and older who qualify by ladder eliminations through their Association and Area. The top area winners participate along with the winner of the Youth Championships who does not qualify for the international team as well as the top Military sailor and the winner of the Leiter Trophy. The top area winners often are eligible for funding and boats are provided for the finals. Housing arrangements can be made through the regatta committee or competitors may stay with their families in local hotels.

The US SAILING/ROLEX Junior Sailing Team
Created in 1989 through a grant from Rolex Watch USA to help recognize the achievements of the top junior sailors in the country. Winners of the following championships are included on this 26 person team along with specially selected or voted upon Sportsperson from the junior world.
1. Winners from the Nautica/US SAILING Youth Championships (all classes)
2. Winners From the US SAILING/Rolex Junior Championships (Sears/Bemis/Smythe trophy winners)
3. Winners from the US SAILING/Rolex Junior Women's Championship (Nancy Leiter)
4. US SAILING/Rolex Windsurfing Junior Championship winners

For other specific information about junior and youth sailing opportunities, contact the following people:

For information about junior programs in your area or on how you might become more involved with junior sailing contact:

Joni Palmer
Sailing Consultant
1187 Green Holly Dr.
Annapolis, MD. 21401
(410) 757-9586
FAX (410) 626-8423

For information about instructor training, community sailing opportunities or ways you might set up a program for junior sailing in your area, contact **US SAILING** direct.

(401)849-5200

For Information regarding the *CISA program and clinic contact*:

Marilee Goyan c/o CISA
PO Box 17992
Irvine, CA 92713-7992
(619) 729-5157
FAX (619) 729-8817

AFTERWORD

I hope that you have enjoyed reading this book as much I have enjoyed writing it during the past year of preparing the manuscript. I know that there is more material here then you can possibly absorb in a single reading, and the book should be used as a reference guide to be looked at over and over again. But in summary, I think that kids and parents may agree on how sailing, as a recreational activity, can enrich one's life.

A Final Word On Where Sailing May Lead:
1. Acceptance to college.
2. A possible career path in sail making, nautical architecture and design or even engineering.
3. A life long hobby which may extend well into adulthood.
4. Development of teaching skills and a great summer job (and tan).
5. Travel opportunities to many regattas around the country and around the world.

For those readers who may wish to learn more about sailing, there is a nice comfortable way to do so by watching some of the many exciting videos which are available. Some of the better ones include a series put out by **US SAILING** titled *Learn To Sail Videos* with topics ranging from beginning sailing, to lines and knots, to sailing fast, or man overboard recovery. There are also some wonderful sailing videos available at your local marine store or marine catalog dealers including Armchair Sailor, Bennet Marine, Boat US, or West Marine Products. Contact your closest dealer and ask for a list of current videos and share the experience with your child.

This volume is intended to become an interactive work with increasing clarity and focus with each new printing. To accomplish this, I am asking that readers send in your experiences so that we might include new chapters with information that is updated and applicable to the changing world we live in. Drop us a line anytime, and we will be happy to respond with your comments.

The Center Press
638 Lindero Canyon Rd. Suite 331
Oak Park, CA 91301
Or FAX us at:
FAX (818) 879-0806

Also, for those of you who wish establishing a sailing program in your area and do not know how to go about starting one, contact **US SAILING** with your questions. They will be glad to steer you in the right direction. There are many ways you can become an involved family in the sport of sailing. You just need to know where to begin.

We hope to hear from as many of you as possible regarding your successes.

Index

470 50
A Fleet 17, 17, 32
abdominal strength 90-91
All American 17
alternative penalty 64
American Sailor Magazine 51, 53, 111
anxiety and stress 85-86
Area A 108, 109
Area B 108, 109
Area C 108, 109
Area D 108, 109
Area Directors 107
Area E 108, 109
Area F 108, 109
Area G 108, 109, 112
Area H 108, 109
Area J 107, 108, 109, 112
Area K 108, 109
Area Orgaization 112
Artof, Jason 8, 96-97
Artof, Lindsay 8, 105-106
Artof, Paul 7, 57
ASBCYC 112
ASMBYC 112, 113
assistant instructor 24
Association Of Santa Barbara Channel Yacht Clubs 112
Association Of Santa Monica Bay Yacht Clubs 112
B Fleet 17, 19, 32
Baumeister, Roy 69
Berglas, Steven 69
burgee 34, 116
burnout 79, 85-86
C-Scows 50
California Yacht Club 47, 71
Camacho, Chris 8, 87
capsize 34
cardiovascular fitness 87-88, 90
chalk talk 2t, 90, 98
chase boat 26
CISA 97, 115, 119
CIT 24, 25
Club/Collegiate Flying Juniors 12, 14, 17, 47, 50
Collegiate 420 12, 14, 17, 50

123

Collegiate Sailing　16-18, 50
Collegiate Sailing Districts　16
committee boat　35, 57-65
Conner, Dennis　13
course chart　35, 57-65
CPR　24, 99
Cressy Cup　19
daggerboard　36, 48
Del Rey Yacht Club　22,23, 47, 96,105-106,112,114
Diskant, Marin　10
DNF　36
DNS　36
dolly　36
doublehanded　12, 43
drugs/alcohol　30, 76
dry suit　36, 37, 53
Durocher, Leo　67, 68
duct tape　37, 52
earthquake preparedness　27, 93
El Toros　12, 49
emergency medical　27
emergency plan　27
equipment needs　26, 51-52
Europe Dinghy　49
Fireballs　50
first aid　24, 92-93, 99
first aid kit　26, 93
fitness　87-94
flexibility　88-89, 92
foul weather gear　37, 52-53
goal setting　80-81
Good, Lois　71
Governor's Cup Match Race　116
Goyan, Marilee　119
Gulfport Yacht Club　56
Harding, Tonya　67, 68
head instructor　24, 30
heatstroke　93
high school sailing　18
hiking pants　38, 52
Holders　50
hypothermia　52
ICYRA　16
Indian Harbor Yacht Club　112
instructor　24, 95-104
International Yacht Racing Union　58, 62
Interscholastic Sailing Organizations　19
ISSA　19

IYRU 58, 62
J-22 50
J-24 50
jib 13, 39, 49
Junior Activities Coordinator 25
Junior Anchor Program 110
Kerrigan, Nancy 67, 68
King Harbor Yacht Club 47
ladder events 108
Larks 50
Laser II 12, 14, 15, 47, 49, 56, 59
Lasers 12, 17, 20, 47, 49, 55, 59, 78
Level 1 Training 24, 97
Level 2 Training 25
life jacket 39, 52, 57
Lightenings 50
losing 67, 84-85
low point scoring 65
Luders 50
mainsail 12, 13, 40, 43, 49
Mallory Cup 19
Marine Tex 40, 54
Massachusetts Bay Trophy 118
mental preparedness 82-83
mental zone 83
military pull-up 91
military push-up 91
modeling 74
moral behavior 71, 72-73
multiple crew sailing 50-51
muscular strength 88
Musselman, Bill 67, 68
Nancy Leiter Clagett Trophy 117
Nautica/US SAILING Youth Championships 81, 96, 116
O'Day Trophy 112, 116, 118
One Design 40, 58
opening day 115
Optimist 12, 48, 49
organization 80
Palmer, Joni 48, 119
parent involvement 21
parent of the day 22
performance anxiety 82, 85-86
Personal Floatation Device 39
PMS 31, 41
program director 25, 30, 47
protest 41, 59, 63, 83
protest committee 64
protest flag 64

race chart 59
race committee   59, 64
race course 59
race preparedness   57-58
racing cones   61
race rules   62-63
radial rigged Laser   49
Red Cross Certification   24
red flag   64
red shirt   17
regatta   41
reinforcement   73, 75
right of way   62-63
rules   58
Rules Of The Road   12, 42, 62
Sabot   12, 47, 48, 49, 66, 70, 105
Sailing Areas   108
Sailing Councils   108
sailing gloves   53, 58
sailing instructions   42, 59
Sailing Instructions   59
Sailing organizations   107-119
Sailing World Magazine   17, 111
San Diego Yacht Club   13, 25
Santana 20   50
Scholastic Sailing   16
Schrof, Joannie M.   70
scoring   64, 65
SCYA   7, 22, 114
SCYYRA   114-115
Sear Bemis Smythe Trophy   81, 112, 116
Seashells   12
self esteem   71, 72-73
self handicapping   69
Shields   50
singlehanded   12, 43
skipper's meeting   43, 59
Snipes   50
Solings   50
sound   61--62
spinnaker   13, 35, 43-44
sports injury   92
sportsmanship   67-77, 83-84
spray suit   53
staff conduct   29
strength   90
stress reduction   85-86
stretching   92
Sunfish   12, 49

Tasers   50
Team Nautica   118
Techs   50
Thistles   50
TMR   73-75
tow line   45, 59
trailers   55
training boats   48
travel tool box   54-55
traveling   54-55
UC Irvine   17, 97, 103
upper body strength   91
US News and World Report   70
US SAILING   19, 24, 25, 49, 51, 58, 59, 62, 71, 76, 107-119
US SAILING Directory   110
US SAILING Membership   110
US SAILING Singlehanded Championships   118
US SAILING/ Rolex Junior Championship   96, 112, 116
US SAILING/ Rolex Junior Sailing Team   112, 119
US SAILING/Rolex Junior Windsurfing Championships   117
US SAILING/Rolex Junior Women's Championship   117
USSF (United States Sailing Foundation)   111
USYRU   8
venue   59, 60
Wainer, Claudia   8, 79
Wells, Peter   96
Westlake Yacht Club   47, 114
wet suit   37, 52, 53
Whitbred Race   13
winning   67-77, 79
women's sailing   22
Y Flyers   50
Yacht Clubs   113
Your Own Worst Enemy   69, 70
Youth Championships   56
YRA   107
YRYSC   114
zero tolerance   30
Zone   83

LEE COUNTY LIBRARY SYSTEM

3 3262 00139 3161

DISCARD

797.1
A
Artof
Sailing

DISCARD

LEE COUNTY LIBRARY
107 HAWKINS AVE.
SANFORD, N. C. 27330

GAYLORD S